LAWRENCE STONE LECTURES

Sponsored by

The Shelby Cullom Davis Center for Historical Studies
and Princeton University Press
2008

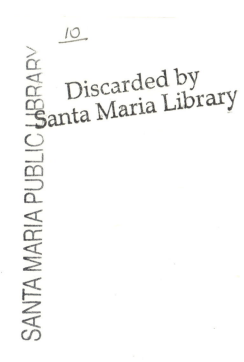

No Enchanted Palace

Mark Mazower

No Enchanted Palace

⤳

The End of Empire and the
Ideological Origins of the
United Nations

PRINCETON UNIVERSITY PRESS
PRINCETON AND OXFORD

Copyright © 2009 by Mark Mazower

Requests for permission to reproduce material from this work should be sent to Permissions, Princeton University Press

Published by Princeton University Press, 41 William Street, Princeton, New Jersey 08540

In the United Kingdom: Princeton University Press, 6 Oxford Street, Woodstock, Oxfordshire OX20 1TW

All Rights Reserved

Library of Congress Cataloging-in-Publication Data

Mazower, Mark.

No enchanted palace : the end of empire and the ideological origins of the United Nations / Mark Mazower.

p. cm. (Lawrence Stone lectures)

Includes bibliographical references and index.

ISBN 978-0-691-13521-2 (hardcover : alk. paper)
1. United Nations—History. 2. Imperialism—History—20th century.
3. World politics—1900–1945. I. Title.

JZ4986.M39 2010

341.23—dc22

2009016699

British Library Cataloging-in-Publication Data is available

This book has been composed in Sabon text with Constantia Display

Printed on acid-free paper. ∞

press.princeton.edu

Printed in the United States of America

10 9 8 7 6 5 4 3 2 1

Contents ∫

Acknowledgments §

I am greatly indebted to Gyan Prakash, the Davis Center for Historical Studies, and the Department of History at Princeton University for the invitation to deliver the 2007 Stone Lectures on which much of this book is based, and for their generous hospitality. I was fortunate enough to get to know Lawrence Stone in his last years at Princeton, and I feel honored to be able to offer this small tribute to him. I am grateful to Princeton University Press for their support of the lectures and of their publication, and to Brigitta van Rheinberg in particular for her attentive readings of successive drafts and many insightful suggestions. Chapter 2 was originally delivered as the 2008 Tsakopoulos Lecture at Columbia University, and my thanks go to Kyriakos Tsakopoulos for the invitation to deliver that lecture. I should also like to acknowledge the help I received in thinking through these issues from among others Cemil Aydin, Duncan Bell, Manu Bhagavan, Alan Brinkley, Partha Chatterjee, Saul Dubow, Marwa Elshakry, Sheldon Garon, Nicolas Guilhot, Peter Mandler, Scott Moyers, Samuel Moyn, Phil Nord, Susan Pedersen, Derek Penslar, Carne Ross, Mira Siegelberg, Anders Stephanson, Helen Tilly, and Stephen Wertheim. Discussing these issues with my students at Columbia and at seminars at the Center for International History has in some ways helped most of all.

No Enchanted Palace

§ Introduction

> We cannot indeed claim that our work is perfect
> or that we have created an unbreakable guarantee
> of peace. For ours is no enchanted palace to
> "spring into sight at once," by magic touch or
> hidden power. But we have, I am convinced,
> forged an instrument by which, if men are serious
> in wanting peace and are ready to make sacrifices
> for it, they may find means to win it.
>
> —Remarks by Lord Halifax, British ambassador to
> the United States and acting chairman of the UK
> delegation, San Francisco, 26 June 1945

"A new chapter in the history of the United Nations has begun." With these confident words, Secretary-General Boutros Boutros-Ghali greeted the end of the Cold War and hailed the "extraordinary opportunity" it presented his organization. The decades-long standoff between the superpowers had marginalized it, but the collapse of the USSR offered the UN not only challenges but renewed meaning. Its peacekeeping role could now be expanded and the mandate for its soldiers made more robust. It could take an active role not only in resettling refugees from war-torn states but also in facilitating political reconciliation, rebuilding bureaucracies, and supervising elections. Also to the UN would fall the mission to oversee global social and economic development, and to provide assistance and advice to the world's poor. And only the UN had the legitimacy to defend human rights robustly and intervene in its members' affairs on behalf of humanity at large. "The Organization," the UN's 1992 *Agenda for Peace* confidently proclaimed, "must never again be crippled as it was in the era that has now passed."[1]

Here was the dream of a new founding moment—as if the world had turned back the clock to the hopes of 1945. Yet if such an opportunity really existed, it was gone almost at once. Civil wars in the Balkans and Africa, and above all the genocide in Rwanda in 1994, provoked critics to fume at the UN's impotence. A series of high-level initiatives designed to reform the organization since then have run aground, while new and previously unimagined layers of internal corruption came to light. Prodded by the Clinton administration, NATO bombed Kosovo without Security Council approval, setting a precedent in which the UN was bypassed in the name of humanitarian intervention. In the new millennium, the administration of George W. Bush advanced a national security doctrine whose advocacy of preemptive war marked an unabashed repudiation of the basic principles on which the UN had been founded. Under Ronald Reagan, the United States had earlier weakened ties with the International Court of Justice; now it also turned its back on the new International Criminal Court, and it undermined international arms control regimes as well as efforts to reach a legally binding agreement for biological weapons. Although it paid lip service to the UN in the run-up to the attack on Iraq (mostly in order to help its ally, the UK government), the Bush presidency could scarcely mask its disdain for the organization: the war, it was clear, would go ahead whatever the UN said or did. But it was not only the unilateralists in Washington who thereby lost faith in it. For much of the rest of the world, overwhelmingly opposed to the idea of invasion, the UN failed too—to defend the principles of multilateralism and collective security. One thing was clear: the high hopes invested briefly in it as the center of a new global order had completely vanished.[2]

Today there is no shortage of proposals to reform it. Some want it to be streamlined to allow fast military action against rogue states and other international outlaws: maybe the Security Council can be enlarged, the veto power of the permanent members weakened, the idea of a UN military staff resurrected. Others feel it should move more toughly against human rights offenders among its own members and do more to stamp certain values—freedom, for instance, and democracy—on the world before it is too late (and, though the fear is rarely voiced, before the Chinese take over). There is the call for it to promote something called "human security"—a blend of development goals and rights—and to claim the right to intervene in defense of the world's citizens when their own governments maltreat them. Yet the suspicion that it is basically too far gone for any reform to restore it to a central role in international affairs is pervasive. Few people seem to feel that the world would be a better place if the UN disappeared (though an American conservative think-tank did publish a 1984 study entitled *A World without a UN: What Would Happen If the United Nations Shut Down*). But few have much confidence in it either. Influential foreign policy pundits talk about creating an Alliance of Democracies instead to get things done when the UN, stymied by authoritarian powers in the Security Council and bogged down by despots in the General Assembly, is unable to act in order to bolster what they call "the democratic peace."[3]

This is a discussion about the UN's future place in the international system. But inevitably it rests on an understanding of its past. Indeed, the intensity of present disillusionment is closely linked to a sense of despair at how far it has fallen short of the standard supposedly set by its founders. Secretary-General Boutros-Ghali justified his expansive 1992 vision of what the UN should do as a way of belatedly realizing "the lofty goals . . . originally envisaged by the charter." Critics agreed. The UN's rules had long been in abeyance; said one commentator, defending U.S. policy in the spring of 2003, "There had been no progress for years." The international system, he went on, had simply developed in a way that condemned the UN to fade into irrelevance, or at best, "to limp along." The Bush administration was harsher still. It foresaw the UN headed for complete irrelevance—just like the League of Nations between the wars—if it failed to get tough with Saddam Hussein: the invasion of Iraq was, it claimed, adverting to the 1930s, its Abyssinia crisis, or perhaps even Munich.[4]

Yet the historical understanding implicit in this entire debate is astonishingly jejune. A great deal is assumed about the UN's past by both supporters and critics on the basis of cursory readings of foundational texts, and there is very little acknowledgement of the mixed motives that accompanied their drafting. Even the available scholarly accounts of how these texts emerged are vitiated by a heavier than usual dose of special pleading and wishful thinking. In them, internationalism is generally presented as something positive, and globalization is depicted as *the* current of modern history. Their guiding assumption seems to be that the emergence of some kind of global community is not only desirable but inevitable, whether through the acts of states, or nonstate actors, or perhaps through the work of international organizations themselves, staffed by impartial and high-minded civil servants.[5]

There is a good reason for this partiality. For many years historians of the postwar international order simply ignored the subject of the UN; for students of the Cold War in particular, and American foreign policy, it seemed marginal if not irrelevant to the main story.[6] What brought it back into focus was first the "new world order" proclaimed by President George H.W. Bush as the Cold War ended, and then, with much greater urgency, and in a very different spirit, the shocked intellectual reaction to the foreign policy of his son. It was Bush II above all who prompted many historians to try to show why the UN matters—or at least, why it did once to the United States. Thus they saw it as their job to provide accounts of American internationalism and far-sighted multilateralist statesmanship as a means of criticizing the nationalistic Vulcans in the Bush cabinet. Franklin Delano Roosevelt, so the story generally goes, paved the way for the United States to provide global leadership in the early 1940s, and advanced the right kind of American values to garner international support. Drawing worthy lessons for the present has thus involved highlighting a contrast between the blinkered unilateralists of the early twenty-first century and the wise and prudent internationalists of 1945. Soon the protagonists of these accounts turn into visionaries and heroes—inspirations for our drabber and less strenuous times: Eleanor Roosevelt, Raphael Lemkin, Rene Cassin, and other leading figures in the emergence of the UN and especially of its human rights regime are now routinely invoked as reminders of what individual commitment and activism can accomplish.[7]

Utopias are not to be ignored, and the utopianism that has attached itself to international bodies like the United Nations and its predecessor, the League of Nations, was certainly a vital aspect of their appeal. It gave them energy, support, and in certain circumstances valuable political capital. But when historians confuse the utopianism of their subject with their own it is easy to be led astray. Reading what one wants back into history is an ancient practice, and today's human rights activists and advocates of humanitarian intervention are not the first to do so. But what has appeared over the last few years is a body of literature that gives a very one-sided view of what the UN was set up to do and generates expectations that its founders never intended to be met. The result is, if anything, to deepen the crisis facing the world organization and to obscure rather than illuminate its real achievements and potential.

At this point, what we need is to take a more critical look at what the UN's founders actually had in mind and to take less for granted about how it started out or what it would become. When we turn back to the 1940s, warning-bells should go off, for we find that commentators then expressed a more wary view of the new world organization than historians currently tend to. Indeed many left the founding conference at San Francisco in 1945 believing that the world body they were being asked to sign up to was shot through with hypocrisy. They saw its universalizing rhetoric of freedom and rights as all too partial—a veil masking the consolidation of a great power directorate that was not as different from the Axis powers, in its imperious attitude to how the world's weak and poor should be governed, as it should have been. Insiders discreetly confided not dissimilar views to each other or to the privacy of their diaries. For the British historian and civil servant Charles Webster, heavily involved in drafting the Charter, it was "an Alliance of the Great Powers embedded in a universal organization," and its key achievement was to have improved the machinery governing relations between the powers. Gladwyn Jebb, Webster's superior, cynically praised the ability of his American colleagues to "delude" human rights activists at San Francisco into thinking "that their objectives had been achieved in the present Charter." This, as we shall see, is only half the story: because they are so rarely united, the great powers did not, and do not, always have their own way. But it is a valuable corrective to the wishful thinking that has passed for historical analysis in the past few years.[8]

The implications for any attempt to read today's concerns back into the formation of the UN are profound. Texts do not speak for themselves, certainly not such bitterly contested texts as the UN's originary documents. One can view the Charter and especially its preamble, along with the Universal Declaration on Human Rights and the Genocide Convention, as testifying to the foundational imperatives of the new world order established in the fight against Nazism. Or one can read them as promissory notes that the UN's founders never intended to be cashed. Their ambiguities should not be ignored. Indeed, several recent critics of the new idealist historiography point to the sheer implausibility of trying to trace the roots of our current humanitarian activism back to the mid-1940s, when talking about human rights was—for the key policymakers—often a way of doing nothing and *avoiding* a serious commitment to intervene. A. Brian Simpson has thus shown that it was not through the Declaration and the UN, but via the later, regionally focused European Convention on Human Rights that a muscular rights regime first emerged. Samuel Moyn has suggested that the modern human rights movement does not date back to before the 1970s at the earliest. And I have argued elsewhere that early UN human rights rhetoric masked the deliberate abandonment by the Big Three powers of serious and substantive earlier commitments to very different kinds of rights regimes. Rights could mean many things to many people. When we remember that it was Jan Smuts, the South African premier and architect of white settler nationalism, who did more than anyone to argue for, and help draft, the UN's stirring preamble, it is surely necessary to be cautious about making our own hopes and dreams too dependent on the stories we tell about the past.[9]

Not that it is only the historians who have failed to do justice to the complexity of the ideas and ideologies that lie behind the UN. Scholars of international relations have been, if anything, even less up to the task. Perhaps, at the most fundamental methodological level, this has stemmed from their anxiety to demonstrate that theirs is a self-contained discipline, capable of generating general theories about world politics. Science envy—for that was what it has amounted to—has led them to idealize the abstractions of game theory and rational choice, and depreciate the role of ideology. This is not the place to explore the impoverished intellectual consequences. What does need to be borne in mind is the way such approaches eliminated the possibility of taking contests of ideas and philosophies seriously in world affairs—as though, for example, the entire epic struggle of the mid-twentieth century between Nazism, communism, and liberal democracy could be explained on the basis of a cost-benefit risk analysis.[10]

But the problem goes deeper. From the start, the professional discipline of international relations—in the shape of the doctrine known as realism—emerged in the 1940s *against* the pretensions of idealistic internationalists, and even at the time commentators such as Walter

Lippmann, George Kennan, and Hans Morgenthau decried the idea of a world organization as a chimera: like some contemporary commentators on the Left today they saw it as nothing more than (at best) a legitimating organ for great power interests. Of course, there is much plausibility in the idea that the UN was designed by, and largely operative as an instrument of, great power politics. Still, this is not the whole story by any means (and Churchill, who had hoped for this was disappointed). More abstractly, even if it were true, it would still remain important to see why certain powers at a certain point in history came to define their security needs in ways necessitating membership of a world body.[11]

During the 1970s, following the collapse of the Bretton Woods system and the erosion of U.S. hegemony, the discipline of international relations did begin to take institutions more seriously. A new approach—known in the trade as neoliberal institutionalism—analyzed what bodies like the IMF, the World Bank, and the World Trade Organization did for their member states and discussed the extent to which they had formed props for the postwar revival of capitalism under American leadership. Scholars therefore now do provide explanations for why states may opt for multilateral rather than unilateral policies, although for the reasons mentioned above they usually do so on the basis of "preferences" among bargaining actors rather than by analyzing ideas or philosophies of multilateralism in their ideological or cultural context. Rather like the post-9/11 historians alluded to earlier, they aim to demonstrate that unilateralism as pursued by the Bush administration runs against the grain of a rational multilateralist tradition in postwar American foreign policy. But revealingly from our perspective, while designed to show American policymakers and other readers why international institutions offer "real" benefits, such scholarship has little to say about the UN specifically. It simply does not regard it as a body of great importance. The political scientist recently appointed director of policy planning in the Obama administration State Department has suggested that transnational contacts across governments and NGOs—not the UN— constitute the real "new world order," and she even looks forward to a "global rule of law without centralized global institutions."[12]

Some of the doubts over the UN may stem from American liberals' mistrust of its ideological diversity. That dictators may rub shoulders there with democratically elected politicians, authoritarian or Communist delegates with liberals and social democrats, strikes them in an era concerned with the universalization of human rights as something less than positive. Social science increasingly employs a sanitized language that banishes overt reference to politics by deploying concepts such as governance, best practice, and the vocabulary of managerialism, but this scarcely hides its authors' deeply rooted value judgments. The so-called liberal democratic peace thesis—based on an argument to the effect that democracies supposedly do not go to war with one another—reflects a common contemporary normative orientation: in this, liberalism is naturalized and presented as the only form of political rationality capable of meeting the challenges of the modern world, and Kant is invoked (though Mill is the real ancestor) to argue for the spread of peace through democracies banding together—and perhaps, even, for some, spreading democracy around the globe. Construed in this vein, American liberalism is rendered unviolent and pragmatic—there is nothing very ideological about it at all—and is soothingly detached from its more coercive legacies of empire and domination. In the words of political scientist G. John Ikenberry, "When all is said and done, Americans are less interested in ruling the world than in creating a world of rules." What is more, they have history on their side for "there is ultimately one path to modernity—and that it is essentially liberal in character." Obama's America may encapsulate very different values from George W. Bush's but in the mind of some of its leading foreign policy theorists, at any rate, it still embodies the World Spirit.[13]

Thus, although multilateralism and democratic cohesion are internationalist ideas that have gained currency across the partisan divide in U.S. politics, far from reconciling Americans to the UN, they have raised further doubts about its value precisely because it is now so far removed from any model of what an alliance of rights-promoting democracies should look like. We may argue over whether the desire to make the world "safe for democracy"—once famously articulated by President Woodrow Wilson—was realized in Bush's unilateralism, or repudiated by it. But even those who think the latter, and still believe in the value of international institutions, regard the UN as a pretty poor vehicle for the projection of freedom. And, in any case, all of this is basically an argument—couched in pseudohistorical and pseudo-scientific terms—about what the direction of American foreign policy should be. For those interested in where the ideological origins of the UN lie, it offers little.[14]

For the latter, Wilsonianism is obviously one point of departure and the first port of call for standard accounts of modern internationalist thought. Yet we should not ask Wilson to bear too much of the posthumous burden of standing for another, better America. As I suggest below, his global stature was not matched by a commensurate ability to articulate a precise program for the international "community of power" he looked forward to. Was he aiming for a new world democratic order, or focusing on what was necessary to bring peace to Europe? Did he believe that national self-determination was globally applicable, and if so, when? Such well-defined American strains of internationalism as did exist—whether radical pacifist, the muscular imperial civilizing mission of Teddy Roosevelt, or the idea of arbitration through international law—he tended to ignore (as do his contemporary revivalists), and the ambiguities in his own thought, if not deliberate, certainly had the effect of allowing successive commentators to pick and choose among his various pronouncements.[15]

I should like to suggest that at least as important as (and for) Wilson and certainly more neglected in the formation of the League, and hence the entire edifice of twentieth-century world institutions, was the contribution of British imperial thought. The British Empire was the world hegemon in the late nineteenth century when the United States was a second-ranking power, and one of the key places where thinking about international organization emerged. What is offered in the following pages is nothing more than the sketch of an argument; it certainly does not aim to provide the whole story of the ideological origins of the League or the UN. But it is a neglected and salutary part of the story, and in some ways, one might even claim, the decisive part—since so much of the world historical interest of both the League and the UN turns out to have lain in their impact on, and involvement in, the endgame of empire.

Specifically, then, this book challenges two interconnected historical axioms: one is that the United Nations rose—like Aphrodite—from the Second World War, pure and uncontaminated by any significant association with that prewar failure, the League of Nations. And second, that it was, above all, an American affair, the product of public debate and private discussion in which other countries played little part. Instead I present the UN as essentially a further chapter in the history of world organization inaugurated by the League and linked through that to the question of empire and the visions of global order that emerged out of the British Empire in particular in its final decades.

For although it could never be publicly admitted during or after the war—the League had become politically toxic by the late 1930s—the truth is that the UN was in many ways a continuation of the earlier body. State Department officials meeting to draw up the outlines of the new postwar organization in the spring of 1942 found Jan Smuts's 1918 pamphlet outlining the League "surprisingly apt today," while many of the experts involved, such as geographer Isaiah Bowman or mandates guru Benjamin Gerig, had been heavily involved in the earlier experiment. The influential American think group—the Commission to Study the Organization of the Peace—which played an important role in helping draft wartime ideas in Washington, had basically been set up at the end of the 1930s by Wilsonian internationalists associated with the League of Nations Association. One CSOP member, John Foster Dulles, used to the intensity of discussions in the United States, found "virtually no thinking about a revived League of Nations" in wartime London. But that was not true; in Whitehall many of those policymakers coming up with proposals for a new world organization were the same men who had been involved establishing the League the last time around. The example of the League of Nations "dominated all the discussions on the drafting of the Charter of the United Nations" noted Charles Webster, in his 1946 Creighton Lecture.[16]

Not surprisingly, therefore, what emerged after the Second World War bore no resemblance to any of the alternative models that circulated—neither a system of powerful regional councils with a small coordinating center run by Roosevelt's "Four Policemen," nor a world government run by civic-minded rights activists or technocrats, nor the alliance of democracies some briefly toyed with. It was basically a warmed-up League—an association of states—and its main novelty was the priority attached to the principle outlined by Webster in 1944, that "the entrance of the United States and the USSR into a permanent organization is more important than the exact form of the organization itself." Following the Dumbarton Oaks conversations, the *New York Times* hailed "the return to the idea of a League of Nations, to be called the United Nations."[17]

Doing what was necessary to keep the wartime alliance of the Big Three together into the peace was its major point of differentiation from the League: the veto power granted them and the other permanent Security Council members was the result. Important consequences flowed from this, of course. The great powers were simultaneously both more willing to support the UN—since it could not act against them—and more willing to ignore it (for the same reason). And there were other differences too—the abandonment of collective rights; the greater respect for nationality; and the waning confidence in international law as an impartial expression of civilization. But the League and the UN bore a close resemblance to one another, and it was understandable that a leading American congressional supporter, Senator Arthur Vandenburg, should have referred to the latter as "a new League," and that Maurice Hankey—perhaps the most powerful British civil servant in the first half of the twentieth century—should have described the 1943 Moscow Declaration on the new world organization as sounding "very like the League of Nations."[18]

As for the central position of the United States in setting up the UN, this too was something of an optical illusion. Not that Washington was not the driving force in this matter during the war: neither Whitehall—where Churchill was still thinking in terms of European stabilization through enforced disarmament—nor Moscow (which largely followed the Anglo-American lead for the sake of great power understanding) were nearly as involved or important. Several authoritative works naturally therefore trace the history of wartime policy preparation back to the United States and testify to the energy and effort that American civil servants expended on getting the new world organization right. But if we take the view that much of the effort of American planners in the Second World War was essentially involved in revising the League system, and if we bear in mind that many of the proposals of lower-level American internationalist policymakers were simply ignored or repudiated by Roosevelt and Truman and never shaped what emerged, then we need to go further back in time to understand where we ended up. Here is where the British imperial dimension enters as a key strand of early twentieth-century internationalism. The UN's later embrace of anticolonialism—discussed here too—has tended to obscure the awkward fact that like the League it was a product of empire and indeed, at least at the outset, regarded by those with colonies to keep as a more than adequate mechanism for its defense. The UN, in short, was the product of evolution not revolution, and it grew out of existing ideas and institutions, their successes and failures as revealed by the challenge of war itself—the Second World War, the First, and further back still, the Boer War at the turn of the twentieth century. To understand how the UN started out, then, we need to begin not in Washington, and certainly not in the early 1940s, but with the debates about international order, community, and nation that were taking place at the start of the century in the heart of the world's leading power, the British Empire.[19]

It is from such a perspective that this book offers a series of probes into the ideological prehistory of the United Nations and the postwar world order. For comprehensive studies of wartime planning and of the diplomacy that surrounded the UN's emergence, or for institutional histories of the world body itself, the reader should look elsewhere. Instead, I proceed by exploring a number of key individuals and their thought. The book opens and closes with two of the outstanding statesmen of the late phase of the British Empire—Jan Smuts of South Africa and Jawaharlal Nehru of India. Between them, their UN experiences define the rise and fall of the idea of an imperial internationalism, articulated by Smuts in the aftermath of the Boer War and definitively demolished by Nehru in a series of policy moves between 1946 and the mid-1950s. In between, two studies of second-tier thinkers show how their writings made explicit many of the assumptions of their age and revealed some of the contradictions. One of these was perhaps the best-known theorist of interwar internationalism, Alfred Zimmern, whose career spans the liberal reaction to the Boer War at one end, and the American deployment of the UN in the Korean War at the other and whose thinking illustrates precisely why liberal supporters of international cooperation tended to become disillusioned with the results. The other chapter focuses on the mid-1940s and explores the wartime

thought of two Jewish social scientists—the lawyer
Raphael Lemkin, and the demographer Joseph Schechtman—in order to show how their analysis of the war
contributed to a complete sea change in postwar attitudes toward national self-determination, international
law, and minority rights—attitudes that would be reflected in the actions of the new world body. Cumula-
tively, these studies, which connect the world of diplomacy to that of intellectual and cultural history, are
designed to help sketch out a rather different perspective on the formation of the world of the United Nations than the one we are accustomed to.

My starting point is a question: What to make of the
fact that Jan Smuts, the South African statesman, helped
draft the UN's stirring preamble? How could the new
world body's commitment to universal rights owe more
than a little to the participation of a man whose segregationist policies back home paved the way for the
apartheid state? Smuts, exponent of racial superiority,
believer in white rule over the African continent, casts
an enigmatic shadow over the founding of the new
United Nations Organization at the end of the Second
World War. Yet it was not a shadow many people at the
time gave any sign of noticing. One who did was the
veteran African American activist W.E.B. Du Bois who
had earlier slammed Smuts for presiding over "the worst
race problem of the modern world."[20] But almost no

one else felt any awkwardness and certainly not Smuts himself. He was a fervent supporter of the idea of international organization, and a believer in the UN.

This commitment of his grew out of many years of thinking about how to make nationalism compatible with broader international affiliations of sentiment, loyalty, and interest. His role in the making of the new South Africa had actually been critical. Mindful of the way the North American colonies had broken away at the end of the eighteenth century, and wishing to keep other white settler colonies (notably his own Union of South Africa) within the safety of the empire's embrace, Smuts and other theorists of the British Empire had turned to the concept of commonwealth to imagine a way of unifying nations in a common cause for the sake of democracy. In his view, South Africa needed to remain within the empire, not only for its own safety but in order to carry out its mission as bearer of civilization to the Dark Continent. The commonwealth idea offered not only a template for this but a way of imagining a new world organization.

As Britain fought the First World War and struggled to secure active American backing, imperial self-interest was grafted onto Wilsonian rhetoric. Smuts himself became a leading wartime theorist of international order, and he played no small role in shaping the League of Nations and brokering accords between Wilson and Whitehall. He was convinced of white racial superiority and believed international organizations should ensure that white leadership of the world continued (rather as Henry Stimson, later Roosevelt's secretary of war, sought to defend "the Caucasian civilization of Europe"). The League itself was an eminently Victorian institution, based on the notional superiority of the great powers, an instrument for a global civilizing mission through the use of international law and simultaneously a means of undergirding British imperial world leadership and cementing its partnership with the United States. After the League collapsed in the 1930s, making sure that the United States would join in a similar organization the next time round became an imperial priority. Smuts was satisfied that the UN represented an improvement on the League because it would keep the United States and the USSR as members while helping the British Empire carry on its civilizing mission in Africa. There was not the slightest hint, in his mind, of the empire's imminent disintegration. A democratic imperial order had been preserved, thanks to the formation of the UN, even as fascist militarism had been defeated. The work of civilizing inferior races, and keeping them in order, could continue.[21]

Smuts's pronouncements were shot through with a sense of moral righteousness that was characteristic of his epoch (not to mention our own). Indeed it was his appeal to a higher morality that constituted his main contribution to the preamble to the UN Charter. In chapter 2, I take this moralizing seriously and ask what pattern of ideas lay behind it, since a fundamental characteristic of first British and then American internationalism has been its powerful and generally unself-consciousness invocation of the language of right. There are a number of thinkers whose views would be worth exploring to

get at this issue. Chapter 2 focuses on one of them—
Alfred Zimmern, a classicist, political theorist, and wartime drafter of the League blueprint in Whitehall.
Through his ideas, I trace how this form of "interna-
tional-mindedness" emerged out of a primarily ethical
conception of community that trusted more in education and the transformation of men's minds and souls
that it did either in law or in institutions. Smoothly
blending the ancient Greeks, Hegel, and a secularized
Christianity, Zimmern placed his faith in "civilization"
and the values of British liberalism, and refused to believe men of goodwill could make other ideological
choices. But this gamble on the future was bankrupted
by the rise of fascism. Once the interwar European crisis
showed Zimmern that Britain's world leadership role
was doomed, he—and others like him—turned instead
to Washington to train the young democracy across the
water in its new global responsibilities. Zimmern told
Americans to see themselves as leaders of freedom and
to regard the United Nations as an instrument for that
greater purpose. And he had a bit part in making it so.
Before the war he had been a key figure in the League's
International Institute for Intellectual Cooperation; in
1945, briefly, he played a key role in the formation of
UNESCO, the body that such believers in the potency of
ideas and education hoped would create the International Mind that would save civilization after 1945 and
contribute to a "moral rearmament" to save the values
of freedom from their new totalitarian enemies. But the
UN was not designed for such a program and when
Zimmern was replaced at UNESCO by the biologist

Julian Huxley, it was a sign that his kind of appeal to a notion of "culture" based on the values of Victorian elite society had been overtaken inside the UN by proponents of a different model of universalism, based instead on deploying science across the ideological boundaries of the Cold War in the service of mankind. Zimmern's moral universalism, which had started out disposing him toward international institutions, ended up by making him impatient with them—much like some of his American political descendants today.[22]

Before the Second World War, imperial internationalism was articulated in a world that took the durability of empire for granted; few, if any, African or Asian nationalist claims to independence seriously registered. The League confined Wilsonian talk of national self-determination almost entirely to Europe and allowed the victorious European imperial powers to expand their informal empires elsewhere. But the possibilities for imperial internationalism, though not instantly disappearing, narrowed sharply in the 1940s. As the struggle with Germany and Japan left the British and other European empires weakened, world leadership passed to the United States. There wartime arguments about the one national group whose fate lay at the heart of the Nazi war—the Jews—showed the shift in attitudes. The Jews were symbols par excellence of the perils of statelessness, and the American debate over their postwar fate showed how thinking about nations had changed. In 1919, anxieties about their plight in Eastern Europe had prompted the creation of the League of Nations minority rights regime. The League had made recognition of new states dependent on their pledging to treat minorities properly and grant them new rights under international law that the League itself monitored. During the Second World War, that regime was decisively repudiated. The Nazi New Order helped undermine it, creating a global refugee crisis that called for a global response. Upholding the Palestine Mandate and committed to restricting Jewish immigration, the British ceded leadership on the issue of refugees and stateless persons to President Roosevelt who had long seen the world's demographic crisis as an underlying cause of the drift to war.

Chapter 3 explores this subject. It looks at two émigré Jews, Raphael Lemkin and Joseph Schechtman, and considers their ruminations on the postwar fate of the Jews and its international implications. Authors of perhaps the most outstanding wartime studies of the Nazi occupation, they reached diametrically opposed conclusions on the broader issues. The question was whether, as Lemkin wanted, to restore minority rights, and perhaps extend the reach of international legal protections through the successor to the League, or to move in the other direction, and to stop interfering in member states' internal affairs altogether and, as Schechtman implied in his studies of forced population movements, to bring stability by uprooting the minorities themselves. What today's UN reformers call "the right to protect" was thus on the table at the outset—indeed had formed a central part of the work of the League of Nations. In 1945, however, it was rejected: advocates of minority rights lost the argument, and as events in Eastern Europe and

Palestine showed, minorities would find less protection under the United Nations than they had done under the League. Lemkin's 1948 Genocide Convention, often hailed as a stride forward, was in fact a last genuflection to a past in which international law had been accorded more weight than could be allowed in the late 1940s. The United Nations became an even fiercer defender of national sovereignty than the League had been and stringent domestic jurisdiction clauses in the Charter, as objectors at the time pointed out, made "much harder the task of dealing with any future persecution of the Jews." Or, for that matter, other minorities as well. Treating national self-determination as a right was not only liberating; it was also a doctrine that trampled over the rights of others.[23]

Thus minorities disappeared in Eastern Europe, and the states of the region became ethnically far more homogeneous thanks to the uprooting of millions of people. And the same principle was extended outside Europe too. In 1947, the UN General Assembly narrowly approved the partition of Palestine and the creation of a Jewish national state. But this was only the start. In the 1950s and 1960s, the principle of national self-determination was globalized in a startlingly rapid fashion, and the UN turned from being an instrument of empire into an anticolonial forum. Smuts, an architect of the League and one of the authors of the preamble to the UN Charter, suddenly found himself outflanked by this dramatic shift. As early as 1946, South Africa was put in the dock for its treatment of its Indian minority and the General Assembly backed Indian demands for South Africa to justify its policies. Anticolonialism won out, South African claims that such matters were not the UN's concern were ignored, and the result was the first act of assertion by the colonial world against the principles of racial hierarchy and European rule.

The General Assembly's support of the Indian delegation shocked the South Africans and suggested that the new world organization contained within it—however embryonically—the potential to become a very different organization from that envisaged by the wartime great powers. Unfettered by legal considerations—at San Francisco it had been decided that the remit of the domestic jurisdiction clause would *not* have to be decided by international law—the General Assembly marked the triumph of politics over law. (The General Assembly's decision in 1947 not to let the International Court of Justice adjudicate on the fate of Palestine followed the same logic.) Neither the Americans nor the British had wanted any criticism of the South Africans; nonetheless, caught between competing international constituencies, they were unable to prevent it.[24]

India's victory in 1946 was real but double edged. On the one hand, it marked the rise of what contemporaries referred to as "Asia." On the other, it altered very little in South Africa itself and offered yet another reminder that the new international organizations, flexible though they had turned out to be, might not be designed to respond to all of the enormous hopes invested in them. With the Nationalists' rise to power in South Africa in 1948, things got a lot worse for all nonwhites. The General

Assembly, it turned out, could do little in the face of Security Council resistance.

And there was another point too. Anticolonialism and antiracism quickly lost their radical edge once states won independence—at that point they often turned into defenders of the status quo and the Indian government was to resist UN intervention in its internal affairs as strongly as the South Africans had done earlier. The UN expanded further and more rapidly than its founders had thought possible. But it remained suspended between its twin functions as great power talking shop and supporter of national self-determination across the world. What had started out as a mechanism for defending and adapting empire in an increasingly nationalist age has turned into a global club of national states, devoid of any substantial strategic purpose beyond the almost forgotten one of preventing another world war. Freezing intact the power configuration at the end of the last one, it looks—so far in vain—for a political raison d'être more suited to the needs of the present.

1
Chapter

Jan Smuts and
Imperial Internationalism

In the closing days of the Second World War, the representatives of fifty nations—led by the Big Three victors over Nazism—met in San Francisco to establish the United Nations as a permanent peacetime organization. Field Marshal Jan Smuts, the South African prime minister, was one of the oldest delegates at the conference— he had the unique distinction among those present of having been centrally involved in setting up the League of Nations more than twenty years earlier. Now, like the others there, he was determined that the new organization should not fail as the League had done. On May 1—the day after Hitler committed suicide—Smuts galvanized the delegates in the San Francisco Opera House. "For the human race," he intoned, "the hour has struck. Mankind has arrived at the crisis of its fate, the fate of its future as a civilized world." Victory in the war must be crowned by "a halt to the pilgrimage of death." The alternative, too terrifying to contemplate, was a third global conflagration. He praised the League of Nations, criticizing "the fashion to belittle or even sneer at it," but noted the "spirit of realism" animating those who had drafted the original version of the UN Charter seven months earlier at Dumbarton Oaks. It was reasonable to recognize, as they had done, the special responsibilities of the great powers, and it was right that they had done whatever was necessary to ensure that the latter support the new world body. Smuts had only one reservation: "The new Charter should not be a mere legalistic document for the prevention of war." Rather it should contain at its outset a declaration articulating the lofty values that had sustained the Allied peoples in their bitter and prolonged struggle. This had been above all a moral struggle, of "faith in justice and the resolve to vindicate the fundamental rights of man." His rhetoric soared. The war against Nazism had been waged "for the eternal values which sustain the spirit of man in its upward struggle toward the light."[1]

The peroration was true—as we will see—to Smuts's long-standing suspicion of legalism in international affairs and to the conviction that he shared with many previous supporters of the League of Nations that world peace was essentially an ethical struggle for the soul of man. But it was also a little misleading. Smuts had come to San Francisco uneasy about what he termed its "strong humanitarian tendency" and the attendant possibility of embarrassment for his own country, South Africa. Fortunately for his peace of mind, the doubts soon vanished and publicly he was feted, hailed as the lone leading survivor of the Paris peace conference, and honored by being made president of one of the commissions. The seventy-five-year-old field marshal still cut a trim, upright figure. Straight-backed, fresh from invigorating walks on the slopes of Mount Tamalpais, he possessed abundant reserves of energy. It was not hard to imagine him as he had been four decades earlier, leading his commandos against the British, a copy of Immanuel Kant in his knapsack.

Smuts was above all a figure of empire—of the British Empire at the very height of its global power. The towering figure in South African politics from the time the Boer War ended, he had produced the constitution of the Union of South Africa and helped to ensure the war-torn country's reincorporation into the British imperial system. Between 1910 and 1924 the former Boer leader was constantly in office, the last five years as premier. Then he was minister of justice before leading the country into a second world war as premier for a second time. In a strange twist of fate, the erstwhile guerrilla was clasped to the bosom of the British establishment. He became a trusted member of the Imperial War Cabinet in the First World War, the creator of the British Royal Air Force, and—above all—ideologue for the new British Commonwealth.

And it is just here—in his thinking about the Commonwealth and its wider meanings for the world—that one starts to see Smuts's relevance to a neglected aspect of the spread of internationalism in the twentieth century. If modern colonial empires were the work of a single late nineteenth-century generation, as the historian W. Roger Louis has suggested, Smuts was a leading member of the generation that followed, who sought to prolong the life of an empire of white rule through international cooperation. There is, to be crude about it, a straight—if unexplored—line that takes us from the constitutional reconfiguration of the British Empire in its final decades to the UN. Could it be, in short, that

the United Nations started out life not as the instrument
to end colonialism, but rather—at least in the minds of
men like Smuts—as the means to preserve it?

༄

From the Boer War onward, a trend toward what was increasingly known as "internationalism" had become evident on both sides of the Atlantic. There were in fact
many kinds of internationalism. There were those who
believed in codifying and standardizing international law,
and giving it much greater weight in diplomacy, relying
on states to turn to the lawyers to arbitrate their disputes
and ward off the threat of war. Such ideas were particularly strong on the European continent and in the United
States where successive secretaries of state before 1914
saw this as an issue calling for American leadership. But
in trusting the judgment and impartiality of lawyers, this
approach was too apolitical and elitist to garner much
broad political support and the radicalizing impact of the
outbreak of the First World War left them behind. The
real intellectual future of early twentieth-century internationalism lay rather in the hands of self-professed
democrats, who believed that an expanded suffrage
would take power out of the hands of warmongers and
allow the peace-loving instincts of the masses to assert
themselves. The radical peace movement in Britain and
the United States called for the emergence of an international "civic principle" that would supersede nationalism and guarantee world peace. Today we might call
this cosmopolitanism. Recasting much older evangelical

ideas, figures like the sociologist Leonard Hobhouse argued that humanity should overcome "artificial units of loyalty" like the nation and join in "international union." The American pacifist Crystal Eastman foresaw a trend toward "unnationalism" in which people would—in a Kantian vein—act directly, not through their governments.

Others disagreed profoundly with this approach and wanted to get to the same destination by another route; they felt that nationalism was not bad in itself, merely in the wrong hands. The British radical, J. A. Hobson, a fierce critic of "imperialism," saw "democratic nationalism" as "a plain highway to internationalism." In 1912 he discussed the idea that "a federation of civilized states" might be powerful enough to keep order in the world. In fact, he regarded as "the supreme test of modern civilisation" whether such a federation would be a force for good, or simply "a variant of the older empires," enforcing a parasitic *pax Europaea* on the world rather than acting in the interests of humanity. Hobhouse praised Hobson's imperial federation project, differing in details but suggesting in his turn that a British imperial federation might serve as a model for the world. "Physically the world is one," he wrote, "and its unity must ultimately be reflected in political institutions." Federalism inside the British Empire would lead eventually to a "world state." What is striking is thus the degree to which even the most radical of British internationalists accepted the imperial framework of world politics.[2]

Elsewhere in the English-speaking intellectual world, a rather different group was thinking along surprisingly

similar lines—not so much for the sake of world harmony as out of concern at the state of the British Empire
itself. Among British commentators, there had been
talk of a federation of white settler nations since the
1880s, although this had run out of steam by the century's end amid accusations of impracticality. But as first
the Boer War and then the First World War revealed the
fragility of the British Empire's constitutional arrange-
ments, the topic emerged once more. After the Boer War
ended, many of the new federationists began to think
through the future of the South African colonies and of
Africa in general.[3] The high commissioner, Sir Alfred
Milner, mapped out the future of Southern Africa in
terms of a kind of manifest destiny, seeking to establish
"a great and progressive community, one from Cape
Town to the Zambezi." The clever young men in his
entourage—his so-called "Kindergarten"—were ardent
Hegelians from Oxford with confidence in the power of
the state to create this new political entity; they priori-
tized white union—healing divisions between Afrikaners
and English-speakers in particular—while urging a
tougher line towards non-Europeans. Thus the language
of the civilizing mission now acquired an unmistakably
racial coloration. "The fact is," wrote Lionel Curtis in
1907, one of Milner's most influential young followers,
"we have all been moving steadily from the Cape idea
of mixing up white, brown and black and developing
the different grades of culture strictly on the lines of
European civilization, to the very opposite conception
of encouraging as far as possible the black man to separate from the white and to develop a civilization, as

he is beginning to do in Basutoland, on his own lines." Milner himself spoke of "race patriotism," and regarded "blood" as the glue binding the empire together. One sees in such words, to be sure, the abandonment of belief in assimilation and a more sharply racialized politics; the more important point is that this new racialization of colonial rule formed a key element in the imperial internationalism that was emerging at this time. Unconcerned with the rights of native Africans, Whitehall was deeply anxious about the political claims of its white settler colonies and their sense of nationalism, which it recognized in 1907 when it granted self-governing Dominion status to them. Three years later, the Union of South Africa was formed, a manifestation of the new federal spirit, and Jan Smuts emerged as a leading proponent of a unified South African nationalism.[4]

As he struggled to overcome the trauma of the Boer War and create a new national consciousness back home, Smuts naturally aligned himself with those who promoted internationalism *because* they were nationalists. Nationalism was a real force in the world, and—in his view—a good one in the African context where it brought whites together and promoted their civilizing mission in the Dark Continent. The question was how to make it peaceful, to prevent it leading to instability, war, or what he called "imperialism"—in other words, unregulated landgrabs at the expense of the reasonable claims of other European powers. One answer was to look to the idea of a commonwealth of nations.

Some of Milner's more idealistic and unrealistic disciples took their belief in a strong state to the point of advocating an imperial government—and later a strong world government too. But Smuts's viewpoint was more sensitive to national loyalties and ultimately more influential. He too identified wholly with the idea of British leadership. But he insisted on the need to recognize the empire's member-nations; this was why, during the First World War, he demanded that the autonomy of the Dominions be explicitly recognized. Hoping to unify imperial defense and to get colonial politicians to shoulder more of the burden, Whitehall had been moving in that direction before the war—at the 1907 Imperial Conference it had ceased referring to Canada and Australia as colonies and the term *dominions* was also extended to New Zealand and to South Africa in 1910. The Dominion viewpoint was a special one: increasingly racist, settler politicians well understood the need to band together. Suspicious of Whitehall though they were, the Dominion politician did not feel confident going it alone. Australia and New Zealand could not, unaided, withstand the "Yellow Peril" of Asian immigration, for instance.[5]

As for the new Union of South Africa, the greatest threat to the European mission in its Milnerite incarnation—to civilize the region—was not black nationalism but dissension among whites. The Boer War had shown the danger, and the outbreak of war in Europe in 1914 reopened the old wound: the English supported the government's decision to enter the war on the British side; most Afrikaners did not. Smuts managed to keep the country together, but only by presenting the war as being fought in the name of a higher ideal—not just the old alliances or power politics but a moral struggle to create a better world, a world embodying and preserving the ascendancy of European civilization. For Smuts, the Great War showed just how easily the old alliance politics inside Europe could disrupt Europe's civilizing task outside it. After the war, some new form of international arrangement would have to be reached.

Smuts exploited the war and the formation of an Imperial War Conference to transform constitutional relations between the Dominions and London, boosting the power of the former within an essentially informal organizational framework. But the emergent British Commonwealth of Nations, in Smuts's view—even more than in that of the Australians, Canadians, or New Zealanders, and much more than for most in England itself—would need a still wider League of Nations to keep it together. Smuts believed it was essential to make the British realize their empire would be *better* off, not worse, with a postwar international body to supervise world order and to cement the alliance between Britain and the United States, which would be so necessary to provide leadership. (Twenty years later, he still believed this, arguing that Commonwealth states would back Britain if they were fellow-members of a common world organization but not if they were simply asked to defend the old balance of power.) But the world would be better off too. In 1917, he argued passionately that military victory must be followed by "moral victory" if "military Imperialism" was to be permanently destroyed—an imperialism "which has drifted from the past like a monstrous iceberg into our modern life."[6] Force had to

be replaced by international cooperation in order to
keep the peace, and so Smuts argued, this transition
from force to cooperation could already be seen happening in "the British Empire, which I prefer to call
(from its principal constituent state) the British Commonwealth of Nations."[7] He went on to describe the
Commonwealth as a kind of blueprint for something
even vaster:

> the elements of the future World Government, which will
> no longer rest on the Imperial ideas adopted from Roman
> law, are already in operation in our Commonwealth of
> Nations. . . . As the Roman ideas guided European civili-
> sation for almost two thousand years, so the newer ideas
> embedded in the British constitutional and Colonial sys-
> tem may, when carried to their full development, guide the
> future civilisation for ages to come.

He hailed the British Empire as "the only successful
experiment in international government" and called for
it to be extended on a world scale. What he meant by this
became clearer in 1921 when he joyfully greeted the Irish
settlement and the emergence of an independent Republic of Ireland as another Dominion of the empire: "The
old British Empire has once more proved its wonderful
power of combining, as it does, the complete freedom
and independence of each state with close association in
a worldwide group of free states. It satisfies both the sentiment of nationality and the tendency towards international cooperation which are the two most powerful
forces of our time."[8] In a similar vein, Smuts made it clear
what the real virtue of the British Commonwealth of

Nations was: it did not stand for standardization or denationalization, but "for the fuller, richer and more various life of all the nations that are composed in it." It was, in short, the "only embryo league of nations." In this mighty struggle between reaction and advance, between virtuous empire and vicious imperialism, the Germans were the arch-enemies. Smuts had initially hoped that the Habsburgs might free themselves from the grip of their German allies and conjure up a similarly beneficial commonwealth of national states in Eastern Europe but their rigidity had prevented this from happening. The British, on the other hand, had ensured their rightful predominance by showing that they could turn themselves from an empire into a league of free nations.[9]

From Smuts's viewpoint, the proposed new postwar organization would not only serve to keep the Commonwealth together but it would also cement relations between the two greatest forces for civilization in the modern world, the British and the United States. He saw quite clearly that the former now depended on the latter for its survival. With determination and skill, he therefore shaped his message not only for the British but for an American audience too, and especially for President Woodrow Wilson himself. He hailed America's entry into the war, called for "a League of Peace in the name of humanity," and in an interview with an American journalist quoted Canning's statement of a century earlier that the New World would come in "to redress the balance of the old." The United States, in his view, formed a league of democracies with Britain and France

against "the last effort of old feudal Europe to block
human progress."[10] But its postwar role was no less important. If the League of Nations was to be able to dis-
pose of the territories of shattered empires without too
much international dissent and not make it look like a
carve-up among those empires that happened to have
won, the presence of the United States would be vitally
reassuring.[11]

⌒

In promoting this idea of a league of nations led by
Britain and the United States, Smuts had an uphill task.
British politicians were traditionally cautious about
making permanent international peacetime commitments: some thought all talk of international organization preposterously radical and associated it with socialism or the Fabians. Only a minority really believed
in it. This became clear in early 1917, when Maurice
Hankey, the powerful secretary of the Imperial War Cabinet, drew up the options in a fashion that showed how
marginal the Smuts position actually was. In Hankey's
words, the British could choose after the war between:
(1) "some sort of International Organisation, such as a
league to enforce peace"; (2) "a league of the character
of the Concert of Europe formed after 1815"; (3) "re-
version to . . . the balance of power." Hankey and the
conservatives regarded the first option, which was close
to what Smuts and many lobby groups wanted, as a hor-
rible American idea to be avoided at all costs, and felt
there was no substitute for defending yourself. They

pushed for the third option—the traditional British approach, relying on naval hegemony, careful alliance diplomacy in Europe and the independence of the Low Countries. Yet in doing so, they ignored the political pressure facing a government that was sending thousands to die in the trenches each month. Moreover, their caution was belied by the facts for Britain *had* participated in a conference system for much of the previous century. Rather reluctantly, therefore, the cabinet accepted that it could not espouse a simple return to the diplomatic procedures that many blamed for the war in the first place, and it moved toward the idea of a great power conference system based on the Concert of Europe that had been established in the wake of the Napoleonic wars.[12]

The real debate thus became over whether the new system would represent any more than this, and this is where Smuts was so influential. Considerable discussion of the need to *organize* internationally was well underway in wartime Britain: Leonard Woolf's well-received 1916 book on *International Government* provided a Fabian perspective, and the Round Table group of young Milnerites were promoting their idea of Commonwealth and imperial federation.[13] Drawing on these, and taking advantage of the deep uncertainty inside the cabinet, Smuts circulated an influential memorandum shortly after the German surrender. In his famous "Practical Suggestion," he argued strongly for a version of a peacetime league of nations that represented a considerable departure from the past, going far beyond earlier wartime drafts for a mechanism for guaranteeing the peace and proposing "an ever visible, living, working organ of the polity of civilization." It should have special responsibility for German colonies and the former Ottoman lands through a system of territorial oversight. In addition, it would oversee the abolition of all conscript armies and the nationalization of arms industries. Around an organization loosely based on the wartime conference system, it would offer no guarantees of political independence to its members but offer some kind of effective sanctions to preserve international peace.[14]

It was the most radical proposal to have emerged openly from the heart of the British policymaking establishment—even Lord Robert Cecil, the cabinet's other ardent internationalist, had not been thinking at this stage about anything so far removed from what had emerged after 1815—and there was immediate opposition. In the cabinet, powerful figures like Curzon, Balfour, and Churchill hated the idea of collective security altogether. What about foreigners meddling in British business? And wouldn't British troops find themselves putting out fires all over the world? Meanwhile, empire hardliners like Milner rejected anything that would entangle the empire in Europe but wanted at the same time to ensure closer relations with the United States. Smuts's plan took internationalism much further than any of them wanted to go; its genius was to link it to the questions of Atlanticism and imperial cohesion that they valued.[15]

These arguments were rehearsed at the crucial British cabinet meeting that met on Christmas Eve 1918 ahead of the peace conference in Paris. Smuts's policy offered something for both the Milnerites and the idealists: it took internationalism further than most of the former wished to go, but tied it to the preservation and even extension of imperial power. The prime minister, Lloyd George, characteristically sat on the fence: any League of Nations must be effective, not a "sham"; on the other hand, it could not have independent executive powers. Although Lloyd George praised Smuts, in fact the spirit of cabinet was clear. There was very lukewarm British support for anything more than a permanent conference system and cautious instructions along these lines were therefore given to Smuts when he and Lord Robert Cecil, headed for Paris in early January 1919 to represent the British government on the League question. They had failed to get their way in cabinet. But it turned out not to matter, for Smuts had won over someone far more influential—President Woodrow Wilson. En route to Paris, Woodrow Wilson was now turning his thought to the peace, and he found Smuts's plans very persuasive.[16]

President Woodrow Wilson is the figure more associated than any other in the public mind with the establishment of the League of Nations and the entire development of liberal internationalism in the twentieth century. And indeed one would not want to downplay Wilson's contribution. As far back as the late 1880s he had seen the American model of federalism as a possible model for world order. But it was the war that brought the question of America's role in any peacetime international organization to the fore. In May 1916, as mass movements called for the country to take a more decisive role in establishing the conditions for permanent peace, Wilson told the League to Enforce the Peace that he was in favor of "a universal association of nations" that could "prevent any war contrary to treaty covenants, guarantee territorial integrity and political independence." Even more strikingly, in his Senate address of January 1917 he demanded "not a balance of power, but a community of power; not organized rivalries, but an organized common peace." Before the U.S. entry into the conflict, therefore, President Wilson seemed surprisingly close in his views not to the lawyers who had been so prominent in U.S. administrations in the past few years but to the radical internationalists. Doubtful of the power of international law unsupported by any change in men's minds, he spoke openly of his desire to make a world "safe for democracy" and to speak to the peoples of Europe "over the heads of their Rulers."[17]

Yet once actually in the war, Wilson went quiet and avoided public discussion, fearing it would be disruptive. In private, he started seeing democratization in terms of national self-determination. In January 1918, he announced America's war aims in the famous Fourteen Points, the last of which, true to his new more nationally oriented internationalism, called for "a general association of nations [that] must be formed under specific covenants for the purpose of affording mutual guarantees of political independence and territorial integrity to great and small states alike." In two minds, even in April 1918, Wilson avoided commenting on the League discussions going on in London, telling the press that the time was not right to go into details, and that he wished to avoid alienating Germany by creating anything that looked like an anti-German Holy Alliance.[18]

The real problem was that Wilson did not know exactly what he wanted. It was Smuts who helped him to find out. The team of wartime experts that Wilson had assembled (known as the Inquiry) had prepared abundant information on the territorial settlement in Europe, but thinking about the precise shape of the new peacetime international organization was much less advanced, and Wilson arrived in France with little to guide him beyond a draft dating back to August. Indeed, most of the ideas he introduced at Paris were based either on Smuts or on other British drafts. He agreed to diminish the role of smaller nations, following Cecil's line that "the Great Powers must run the League."[19]

Much in Smuts's view on international politics was bound to appeal to Wilson. Both men were instinctive moralists, idealizing the power of communal ethics over the selfish pursuit of state or sectional interests, convinced above all that the sources of conflict vanished when men of lofty judgment approached things as a whole. The rhetoric of both men could inspire their followers and baffle their enemies. But the key was what to do with the territories of the defeated powers, and their colonies in particular, and here they differed. As the British pro-Americanists like Smuts were keenly aware, American anti-imperialism—whatever that really meant—represented an unmistakable threat to an Anglo-American understanding. Smuts and other Commonwealth theorists hoped to bring the Americans round to their conception of enlightened empire and to make them recognize the limited applicability of the concept of national-self-determination. "In tropical Africa, as in the

Pacific," wrote Lionel Curtis in an influential article, "the only hope of those races who cannot as yet govern themselves of ever learning to do so is in tutelage by some great democratic civilized nation. Once for all, the League of Nations will render obsolete the old pernicious idea of empire, rightly abhorrent to the American tradition." Such thinking influenced Smuts and thence Wilson.[20]

Bridging the gap between Washington and the Dominion was crucial. As it was, the idea of turning former German and Ottoman possessions into League mandates turned out to be an ingenious way of squaring the circle between the British Dominions' demand to annex former German colonies and the need to pay lip service to Wilsonian idealism. Smuts had initially thought of mandates as a way of preparing Eastern European peoples for full sovereignty. But as they took matters into their own hands and demonstrated their strategic importance as a buffer between Germany and Bolshevism, the mandates idea was instead applied outside Europe. Creating the idea of international trusteeships would be, Smuts wrote, a "small concession" for the sake of American support. They would help bring the Americans into an Anglo-American "colonial alliance" that would become "a bond of union . . . between the United States and ourselves." And by watering down oversight clauses and introducing the idea of a third tier of mandates whose terms were all but indistinguishable from outright annexation (or it seemed at the time)—he managed eventually to win Dominion backing. The truculent Australian premier "Billy" Hughes had initially gone all out for annexation of the former German Pacific colonies. But even he retreated when Smuts reassured him quietly that Wilson "has no tangible idea" on the subject of "mandatory control."[21] The Dominions thus got most of what they wanted, including control of immigration, a key issue. Race was much on their minds and although the Japanese received their South Sea Mandate too, their proposal to outlaw racial discrimination was turned down, precisely because it was understood from the start as a challenge to white immigration controls around the Pacific rim.[22]

Meanwhile, the Ottoman lands were divided up between the British and the French; so were the German colonies in Africa. The Italians, Belgians, and Portuguese were sidelined. In British eyes, *they* were the imperialists, unable to separate their own selfish economic interests from the greater good of humanity. Territories had been allocated in the proper fashion, through a diplomatic conference, and the work of civilization could proceed. The British Empire had never been so large, and much of this was thanks to the new international organization that Smuts had been so influential in bringing into being.[23]

⌒

What, then, were the principles underpinning this internationalist reinforcement of empire? The answer can be seen in the context of South Africa itself. In 1917, one week after his important wartime address on "The League of Nations," Smuts gave another speech on "The Future of South and Central Africa" at the Savoy Hotel.

A tribute to what had happened in his homeland since the British victory in the Boer War, it contained what looked like an outspoken attack on racism. Smuts denounced the "arrant nonsense" of "the remarkable doctrine of the pure race" associated with "a Germanised Englishman Houston Chamberlain." This was "the doctrine . . . that the governing races of the world are pure races and that they simply debase themselves and become degenerate if mixed with alien blood." Smuts was scornful. In South Africa, he declared proudly, "We want to create a blend out of the various nationalities and to create a new South African nation out of our allied racial stocks and if we succeed in doing that we shall achieve a new nationality embracing and harmonising our various traits and blending them into a richer national type than could otherwise have been achieved."[24]

Yet this claim was not perhaps what it seems today. For what Smuts was actually talking about was the "white racial unity" that was essential if South Africa was to be made what he called a "white man's land." So far as the black majority was concerned, Smuts sang a very different tune:

We have come to some certain results. You remember how some Christian missionaries, who went to South Africa in the first half of the nineteenth century in their full belief in human brotherhood, proceeded to marry native wives to prove the faith that was in them. We have gained sufficient experience since then to smile at that point of view. With us there are certain axioms now in regard to relations of white and black; and the principal one is "no intermixture of blood between the two colours." . . . It has now become an accepted axiom in our dealings with the natives that it is dishonourable to mix white and black blood.[25]

Smuts put a positive gloss on segregation; it was the price to be paid for civilizing Africa from the South, a reminder of the fact that "the white race in South Africa" had duties as well as rights, and should act as "trustees for the coloured races." But there was an unmistakable note of racial anxiety as well. The war had shown the danger that could be posed in the future by arming natives, and there should be international agreements to prevent this from being repeated. Outnumbered in Africa itself, white settlers needed the protection of empire; secession was thus something Smuts bitterly opposed, a line demarcating the permanent outer limit to the political aspirations of the South African nationalism he wanted to define.

In a student essay written many years earlier, Smuts had predicted that "the race struggle is destined to assume a magnitude on the African continent such as the world has never seen. . . . And in that appalling struggle for existence the unity of the white camp . . . will not be the least necessary condition—we will not say of obtaining victory but of warding off [the ultra pessimists say of postponing] annihilation."[26] After the Great War, such prognoses bled into fears of a global race war and a clash between "West" and "East." The war increased eugenicist and Malthusian concerns, and demographers increasingly saw historical struggle as a problem of fecundity, a grim contest between fast-breeding races of low mental capacity and sluggish races of higher qualities. The American Lothar Stoddard's best-seller, *The Rising Tide of Color against White World-Supremacy,* published in 1922, really caught the international mood. Like Smuts, Stoddard depicted the First World War as a tragically fratricidal struggle "between the white peoples." Stoddard warned that although politically whites had ended up in 1918 in possession of even more of the globe than ever before, in reality, they were overstretched and outnumbered. "The coloured races" outnumbered the whites, two to one; and in any case, most of the latter were cooped up in Europe. To make matters worse, the former were outbreeding the latter, helped by the success of the white civilizing mission in bringing down previously high mortality rates.[27] So far as Africa was concerned, Stoddard noted that unlike in Asia, "the European has taken root." "The crux of the African question" was "whether the white man, through consolidated racial holds north and south will be able to perpetuate his present political control over the intermediate continental mass which climate debars him from populating." For Stoddard, this was a vital question for Europe since Africa was "the natural source of [its] tropical raw materials and foodstuffs."[28]

Smuts was gloomy too about the future of white man's values, but ever the evolutionary idealist, he believed that if empire was sufficiently adaptive and spirited, it still provided the best means of preserving and extending them. In the African context, this meant allowing South Africa to act as the bearer of European civilization by expanding northward. His chief goal in entering the

Great War, after all, had been to gain German South-West Africa for the Union and perhaps the southern part of Portuguese East Africa too. South Africa had expansionism hardwired into its constitution, for as historians have pointed out, the 1909 act that united the country had also divided southern Africa and was not intended to be a permanent arrangement. It had left the High Commission Territories and Southern Rhodesia outside, and actually included a schedule for bringing them in. Smuts himself—like British federalists—had been calling for expansion to the Zambesi and maybe to the equator since 1895, and he certainly was not about to give up now that Germany had been removed from the arena. The whole area of East Africa, he wrote in the 1920s, could "be made into a great European state or system of states during the next three or four generations." In 1929 he called for "one great African dominion stretching unbroken throughout Africa." What was needed was "a resolute white policy" so that there would emerge "a white state in time more important than Australia . . . a chain of white states which will in the end become one from the Union to Kenya."[29]

But in the early 1920s, unfortunately for Smuts, the momentum toward a Greater South Africa hit a series of road-bumps. One problem was the lack of white unity: in 1921, settlers in Southern Rhodesia voted for self-government rather than incorporation, fearing domination by Afrikaners. This in turn made the transfer of Bechuanaland seem less inevitable and its regent, Tshekedi Khama, brilliantly exploited London's concerns about South Africa's increasingly racialized native policy. But the bigger problem was the League of Nations itself, which showed signs of distinct unhappiness at South Africa's administration of its mandate in South-West Africa. The Permanent Mandates Commission in particular, the body charged with watching over the mandates as a whole, took its role more seriously than Smuts or anyone else had expected and actually criticized South Africa for its administration. In 1922 the aerial bombardment of native rebels by South African forces in the so-called Bondelzwaarts massacre left more than a hundred dead, put South Africa in the spotlight in Geneva, and spurred the growth of pronative sentiment in Britain. In 1923, the announcement by the British that Kenya, where white settler interests had always come first, was henceforth to be regarded "primarily ... as an African territory," marked an important shift in Whitehall. It was, not coincidentally, at precisely this time, that "racialism" shifted its meaning in the South African context, no longer primarily denoting relations between English and Afrikaner but rather between blacks and whites. This was the period of Smuts's premiership, when the foundations of the future apartheid regime were being laid by eroding the last remnants of the native suffrage and introducing segregationist settlement restrictions. Smuts convinced himself, if not everyone else, that these measures left blacks as well as whites better off: each had "their proper place" and both had "their human rights." Meanwhile his own party was being pushed down the path toward apartheid as the rise of the Nationalists reinforced calls to eliminate the last vestiges of black electoral rights (in the Cape Colony) and to curtail the native franchise.[30]

Despite his discomfort at the hands of the Permanent Mandates Commission, Smuts remained proud of the League of Nations and convinced of its historical importance. It was a defender of world order in the name of civilization and without it, Europe would "continue to writhe in her convulsions into the blackness of final anarchy." Above all, he was convinced that the League was essential for the empire and Commonwealth. He did not see the check to his expansionist dreams in Africa as a significant reason to abandon his advocacy of the Commonwealth and still regarded the British Empire as a force for good in an increasingly uncertain world.[31]

The regard was mutual. In Britain, despite the growing criticism of South Africa's native policies, Smuts's reputation was as high as ever, and he took advantage of it to promote his racialized version of the civilizing mission. In his 1929 Rhodes Lectures at Oxford he called on young British students to move to Africa to strengthen "our civilization" and save the continent from barbarism. Encouraging English settlers to come to South Africa was of course essential for Smuts's domestic position, as it would weaken the Afrikaners politically, but characteristically he presented it as the path to virtue too. World peace, he told them, could be achieved by expanding the colonial policy of the British Empire under the aegis of the League of Nations. To men like H. G. Wells this sounded old-fashioned and reactionary, and young Leftists were starting to question Smuts's basic premise, that it was possible to be supportive of the League and the empire at the same time. (Only a few years later, the League of Nations Union held a debate on whether "it is possible to be a loyal supporter of the League of Nations Union and remain a staunch imperialist?")[32] But other, older League of Nations supporters (men like the classicist Gilbert Murray) were deeply sympathetic, King George V invited Smuts to stay, and the cabinet asked him to become High Commissioner of Palestine so that he could civilize the Arabs as well as the Africans. Smuts was committed above all to South Africa, however, and first as justice minister (from 1933) and then as prime minister (in 1939), he continued the segregationist line. In accordance with his own personal evolutionist philosophy, he saw the task of the state to provide different groups with rights in accordance with their level of racial competence, or as he put it, "personality." Africans were simply nowhere ready for nationhood, and his job was to persuade the British that the South African policy, increasingly unwelcome to Whitehall, was in fact blazing a path the other colonies should follow as well. To Lord Lugard, the British colonial grandee serving on the League's Permanent Mandates Commission, he confided that he thought segregation the best option for Kenya too.[33]

Yet, although Smuts believed in racial segregation, this was only for Africa and other "uncivilised" regions of the world; it was certainly not for Europe. Anything that divided Europeans he regarded with dismay as fragmenting the continent's cultural unity and threatening its ability to lead the rest of the world toward civilization. It was therefore precisely because of his racism that he saw the emergence of Hitler as deeply alarming (more alarming indeed than Soviet communism). "We shall have our hands full," he predicted in 1932, "saving civilization from shipwreck."[34] By dividing Europeans on racial grounds, and setting aside the rule of law, National Socialism in his view constituted a grave threat to that European ascendancy by which he set such store. This was not so much for South Africa itself—although right-wing extremism did pose a momentary threat there too—as for world order, European unity, and the prestige of Anglo-Saxon liberal values above all. When war broke out in 1939, Smuts did not wish for neutrality: he carried the South African parliament with him and skillfully brought the country in on the British side, even though the white population was deeply split. Even more than in 1914, he regarded this decision as not only morally right but also justifying further expansion. "The efforts you are making," he told South African troops in Kenya in 1940, "will, perhaps not in our time, bring about a United States of Africa." Indeed he was working through the war on a plan for a new "Pan-African" superstate that would stretch right up to the equator, coaxing the "young British states to our north which are our real industrial and political hinterland" into partnership with South Africa. And he still looked forward to asserting control over the High Commission Territories and annexing South-West Africa—a view with some support in Washington.[35]

Characteristically, though, he did not simply annex the mandate, as someone less trusting of the power of international institutions might have done. Instead, fatefully, he waited for the postwar peace conference to press his claim. South African economists provided the customary justification for a takeover: they talked about making the deserts to the north productive through irrigation schemes and settling the country's "surplus" populations there. But Whitehall was not impressed by the timing. "Nothing could make a worse impression," wrote one British civil servant, "than if we were to appear to hand over these Territories in time of war when we were fighting for the interests of small nations." Looking beyond the elderly Smuts, the British worried at the possibility of extending Afrikaner nationalism up through eastern and central Africa.[36]

How, we might ask, could Smuts not have seen which way the wind was blowing? Did he not realize the extent of growing antiracial sentiment in England, and the powerful anticolonialism to be found in the United States. Yet it might be better to ask: which way *was* the wind really blowing? The Atlantic Charter, after all, was a deeply ambiguous document. It was both an international commitment to dismantle the European empires (the American view) and a reaffirmation (for Britain) of the Victorian idea that Europeans were fit for sovereignty and others not. That, at least, was Churchill's reading of it, and whatever the American public might have thought, Churchill always repudiated the idea that it implied any termination of the British Empire, and President Roosevelt eventually gave up insisting otherwise. Of course, like Wilson's Fourteen Points, the Charter was wartime propaganda and acquired meanings in the colonies that Churchill had not foreseen. In South

Africa, for example, the fast-growing African National Congress and others demanded its application. In July 1940, the ANC passed a resolution on the war that supported the Commonwealth but called for full citizenship for Africans. Smuts had initially shown signs of sympathy with this: worried by the course of war and by the Afrikaners' pro-German sympathies, he wanted to shore up African allegiance to the Allied cause. Fearing that the Japanese might invade and arm the blacks, he was driven to contemplate arming them instead. In January 1942, he delivered a speech in Cape Town that criticized the German "idea of a master people" and was widely interpreted as signaling a more conciliatory line in domestic policy.[37] But once that danger was past, he reversed direction and he won the wartime 1943 election in part thanks to his turn to a more hard-line policy. The 1943 ANC memorandum, "African Claims in Africa," was simply rejected by him as a false reading of the Atlantic Charter. To British and American audiences, he reiterated the continued importance of white rule over regional groupings of colonies and warned that in Africa in particular the mandate system had outlived its usefulness. His article in *Life* at the end of 1942, intended to rebut American attacks on British imperialism, called for international collaboration in the development of "backward countries" and recast colonialism as a kind of depoliticized guidance toward higher standards of living. Speaking to members of the Empire Parliamentary Association in London in November 1943, he was even more forthright: there was no general solution for the racial conundrums of the British Empire, and after the war ideals would have to be matched with the realities of power. Any new postwar world organization must recognize the authority of the Big Three. But since British power now rested largely on its empire rather than in any European resources, this must be preserved to preserve a parity of power within "that splendid trinity." British colonial administration would have to show flexibility—in particular, in grouping existing smaller colonies into larger regional federations and other kinds of units. Colonial Africa, he suggested, could be carved into three groups—west, east, and southern—under governors-general, or under the sway of dominions. Clearly Smuts believed the war should bring a Greater South Africa under white rule closer not further away.[38]

At the same time, as so often in Smuts's long career, the domestic ambitions were accompanied by the rhetoric of the visionary, globe-trotting statesman-philosopher, committed to his evolutionist paradigm of cosmic harmony under beneficent white guidance. At the end of 1940, he defined the struggle against Nazism as a sign that "civilization is determined to uphold, and will uphold, the principle that racial domination, racial exclusiveness and top-dogism are in conflict with the whole trend of human progress and enlightenment." Long before Germany had invaded the USSR, and before Pearl Harbor brought the United States in, he called for American intervention and emphasized that a "new peace" would require a "general plan for the world community of the future." In May 1941, the year he was appointed field marshal, he broadcast his vision of the coming "new world order": anchored in Christian ethics, it would be based on associations of states—"for the day of the small independent sovereign state is passed." The British Commonwealth of Nations formed the inner circle of resistance to Hitler; next to this was the United States ("which has the same ethic of life and the same political philosophy"), and finally there was an "outer circle" of free democracies." Collectively, these formed the basis for a future "world society" that could provide "an efficiently functioning organ of the world community. . . . Capable of binding the component nations in the paths of peace and ordered progress and arranging its relations with other States not members of the association." This was the political expression of his own philosophy of holism, an evolutionary creed in which progress was measured through the accretion of individual units voluntarily combining themselves into ever larger wholes.[39]

By then, the planning for a permanent world organization based on the wartime United Nations was well under way. This time round, the British and American positions were reversed, with the British (led by the distinctly unenthusiastic Churchill) relatively slow to enter the planning debate and Washington making the running. If, in the First World War, the paperwork that counted was being done in London, in the early 1940s Whitehall was too preoccupied with survival to worry very much about the future. Inside the U.S. State Department, on the other hand, and outside it too—thanks to revived pro-League groups like the influential Committee to Study the Organization of the Peace—postwar planning was proceeding in detail. There was general agreement that referring to any revival of the League of Nations would be thoroughly unpopular; nevertheless, for many of those involved, it was the League template that provided the model they would refine, modify, and present the world as the proposed United Nations Organization. Obvious alternatives all fell by the wayside: there were few takers, either in the United Kingdom or the United States, for the idea—mooted briefly in the critical early months of the war—for a formal Anglo-American Union to guarantee democratic solidarity into the peace. Once it was obvious that Germany would be defeated such a plan lost its rationale. Nor were there many this time round in London who felt—as Secretary of State for India Leo Amery did—that merely informal cooperation with the United States would be enough. Joint partnership in a continuation of the wartime alliance was the generally agreed way forward.[40]

Smuts was on the margin of these developments but he did follow them carefully and made at least one important intervention, persuading an unenthusiastic Churchill to save the critical four-power talks on the future of the new world security organization that took place at Dumbarton Oaks (outside Washington) in late 1944 by accepting Stalin's view that permanent members of the new Security Council should have a power of veto. For Smuts, it was of overriding importance to get the backing of *all* the great powers for the new peacetime organization; the failure to achieve this, in his view, had been the Achilles heel of the League, which in many respects he otherwise regarded as an excellent model. If the Russians stayed out, he warned, they

would become the "power center of another group" and
"we shall be heading for World War Three." Churchill
saw the point, telling Roosevelt (at about the time that
he and Stalin agreed on a carve-up of the Balkans into
spheres of influence) that "the only hope is that the three
Great Powers are agreed." Indeed this was to become
the precondition for effective leadership of the new
UNO—a precondition that almost from the start was
doomed of course to fail.[41]

Smuts's chief contribution to the United Nations was
yet to come, however. The proposals that emerged from
the Dumbarton Oaks discussions left the rest of the
world distinctly underwhelmed. Bearing in its funda-
mentals a remarkable resemblance to the prewar League,
the proposed new peacetime organization differed in
one important respect only—in the extensive new power
it gave to the permanent members of the Security Council. With no mention made of freedom for the colonies,
and a far more hierarchical structure than the League
had possessed, Dumbarton Oaks was all too obviously
a great power stitch up, couched in a dry bureaucratic
language that failed to capture the imagination.[42]

Here was where Smuts leapt in: it was not that he disliked the substance of what was proposed for the
League's successor (on the contrary, he approved), but
rather that he understood the need for it to win wide-
spread popular acclaim to have any chance of prosper-
ing. At Yalta, in early 1945, the Dumbarton Oaks conversations hardened into proposals to be presented to an
international conference in the spring, the Big Three
managed to agree on voting mechanisms for the Security

Council, and the Americans issued invitations to a conference to be held at San Francisco in the spring to establish the new organization. It was at the meeting of Commonwealth ministers in London shortly before the San Francisco conference in April that Smuts argued strongly that the draft of the Charter needed to be prefaced by something capable of attracting public support. Merging his own outline with a text that had been gathering dust in the British Foreign Office, Smuts won the ministers' backing for his preamble and headed for San Francisco determined to fight for it. There he had the satisfaction of seeing his text adopted unanimously, with a few modifications, as the preamble to the UN Charter itself. Speaking in the closing plenary session as "an old veteran of the wars and of peace conferences," he hailed the Charter as a "good, practical workmanlike plan for peace," but stressed that it would need to be supported by a "total mobilization of the human spirit . . . [by] all the vast network of social and moral agencies which are the support of our civilization."[43]

This was the language of prewar liberal idealism, an approach that took the moral mission of empire for granted. Smuts himself clearly believed this and he publicly praised the United Kingdom to the San Francisco conference as the "greatest colonial power" in the world. "Men and women everywhere," he stated, "including dependent peoples, still unable to look after themselves, are thus drawn into the vast plan to prevent war." President Truman predicted that with the Charter, "the world can begin to look forward to the time when all worthy human beings may be permitted to live decently as free people." If this was a critique of European imperialism, it was one the British—and Smuts—could live with. At San Francisco, dissidents and doubters were silenced or ignored. The Americans sat on the Philippines delegation when it tried to get a commitment to independence written into the Charter; an Ecuadorian proposal to allow a vote by two-thirds of the UN members to lead a colony to independence was also squashed. The Egyptian delegate had been impolitic enough to remind delegates that promises of a new order had been made in 1919 and soon forgotten. His recommendation that the best way to avoid repeating the error was to incorporate into the Charter a commitment to live up to the ideals of the Atlantic Charter—what he described as "a charter for all humanity"—got nowhere. As *Time* noted, the UN Charter was basically designed to ratify a division of the world into "power spheres"; it was, in this respect, a more effective and ideologically more liberal, version of the 1940 Axis Tripartite Pact between Germany, Italy, and Japan, and completely compatible with Smuts's wartime advocacy of powerful regional blocs.[44]

The veteran African American intellectual W.E.B. Du Bois—another veteran of Paris in 1919—was scandalized and pointed out that the proposed international Bill of Rights omitted any mention of colonized peoples. When the American Jewish Committee's proposed declaration of human rights was sent him for signature, he protested that "this is a very easily understood declaration of Jewish rights but it apparently has no thought of the rights of Negroes, Indians and South Sea islanders. Why then call it a Declaration of Human Rights?"[45] Or as he put it more acerbically about the time of Smuts's address at San Francisco: "We have conquered Germany . . . but not their ideas. We still believe in white supremacy, keeping Negroes in their place and lying about democracy when we mean imperial control of 750 millions of human beings in colonies." But much had happened in the four years since Roosevelt and Churchill had met at Placentia Bay, and the future of the European empires was no longer a subject for discussion. On the contrary, the American navy had woken up to the fact that a few Pacific bases of their own might be useful, and wartime American drafts of a declaration of independence of colonial peoples were archived as were thoughts of making a declaration of human rights an integral part of the Charter. Mandates were turned into trusteeships, and colonies became dependent territories, but little seemed to change apart from words, and proposals to commit the new UNO to the eventual independence of all colonies were defeated. "The world has once more returned to a terrific scramble for coloured territories and spheres of influence," wrote a West African journalist at the end of May. "New life has been infused into predatory imperialism."[46]

The British historian and diplomatic adviser, Charles Webster, was—in the privacy of his diary—no less blunt. The United Nations Charter, he wrote at the end of the conference, established "an Alliance of the Great Powers embedded in a universal organization as the Covenant [of the League of Nations] also was." Webster congratulated himself of having found "new methods of harmonizing the Great Power alliance theory and the

League theory." The trusteeships in particular were nothing substantially new. On the contrary, "we have allowed our mandates to go on under the new control but for the rest the matter remains exactly as before except that there is a sort of machinery if states desire to put their colonial territories under it. We have no such intention and I am sure no other power has."[47]

Thus when Smuts's preamble called for the United Nations to "re-establish faith in fundamental human rights, in the sanctity and ultimate value of human personality, in the equal rights of men and women, and nations large and small," he was not committing himself to the dismantling of the segregationist state in South Africa, still less to that of the British Empire as a whole, nor did he see any incompatibility between his rhetoric and his policies. Smuts's conception of "personality" was a fusion of Hegel, Walt Whitman, and evolutionary biology, something that made differential degrees of freedom and differential treatment of groups by the state not merely reasonable but necessary for human progress.[48]

From Smuts's point of view, San Francisco was thus like Paris twenty-six years earlier, only better. Despite anticolonial undercurrents, the Africans had been seen off without a murmur. Small nations had been told to shut up and acquiesce in what the Powers wanted if they wished for any kind of international organization at all, and thanks to Smuts, the Russians remained in. The British were relieved: having tried, and failed, to get the United States to "learn its responsibilities" to backward races in 1919, it looked this time as if they had succeeded. Provided only that the Big Three worked together, the new United Nation Organization—basically little more than an improved version of the old League model—could safeguard the peace and create the conditions for European values to be globalized. In Smuts's mind, the UN Charter contained little that was incompatible with this view of the world; there was no commitment to granting independence to the colonies at all, and the United Nations could emerge, as he intended, as a force for world order, under whose umbrella the British Empire—with South Africa as its principle dynamic agent on the continent—could continue to carry out its civilizing work. Smuts might no longer speak the classicizing language of his youth—when he had talked easily about the mission of "half a million whites" to lift up "the vast dead weight of immemorial barbarism and animal savagery to the light and blessing of ordered civilisation"—but the task was the same as ever. This time, thanks to the new UNO, the white race might succeed.[49]

2

Chapter

§

Alfred Zimmern
and the Empire of Freedom

> We alone do good to our neighbours not upon a
> calculation of interest but in the confidence of
> freedom.
>
> —Pericles in the Funeral Oration, Thucydides,
> *Peloponnesian War*

That strange fusion of empire, liberal internationalism, and moral self-righteousness that Smuts espoused reflected a sense of rectitude and political virtue entirely at ease with the idea of world leadership, hierarchy, and imperial control, capable of seeing the exercise of power as a burden undertaken for the general good and uncomfortable with too frank a recognition of its basis in force. The idea that a stable world order should be morally righteous goes back at least to Immanuel Kant and his vision of perpetual peace, if not to medieval doctrines of natural law or indeed the Hebrew Bible. But if we distinguish between the general vision of a world of different peoples existing at peace with one another and the specific idea of a peaceful system or arrangement of states and peoples, then the roots of moral internationalism turn out to be little more than a century old and closely connected to the changing political and philosophical culture of the British Empire. It was only at the start of the nineteenth century, after all, that Jeremy Bentham invented the conception of the "international" as a realm of governance, and only by the century's end that the unmistakable spread of nationalism as a political creed necessitated sustained reflection on its international implications. Sharing the assumptions of men like Smuts were contemporaries who were less involved in politics and policy but for that very reason perhaps more explicit than he was in articulating the philosophical underpinnings of the liberal internationalist worldview. Like him, they were mostly Oxbridge men, brought up on the classical and philosophical texts circulating in British university circles in the late nineteenth century. They looked to the ancients for perspective on the modern world's problems and defined the task of securing world peace in sweeping historical terms. The creation of new international organizations formed a central part of their approach, but the nitty-gritty of organization itself was not central for them in the way it was for Fabian socialists, and they had little faith in governance alone. In their view, a world body was only the means to a more fundamental end—that of transforming humanity's consciousness and inculcating a new sense of international community based on the perennial values identified by the ancients. Their classicism thus made them supporters of, but not wholehearted believers in, bureaucratic solutions to the problem of world order. The United Nations, like the League before it, garnered their support, but this support was conditional on its ability to meld moral and political global leadership.

This chapter explores the implications and limitations of such an outlook through the thought of Alfred Zimmern. Less well-known than Smuts, Zimmern is one of those men whose ideas, with all their idiosyncrasies, can provide a way into guiding assumptions of an era. Perhaps the preeminent theorist of internationalism between the two world wars, he was a man who crystallized in his writings and life the intimate connection between Victorian readings of the ancients, the moral ideology of British global leadership, and the new liberal internationalism. Starting off as a classicist, Zimmern became briefly a key policymaker during the First World War: in fact, it was he who largely drafted the crucial Whitehall blueprint for the new League of Nations on which Smuts drew in 1918. When he left the Foreign Office he become a pioneer in the professional study of international relations, which he taught on both sides of the Atlantic as well as a leading figure in the League's efforts to establish an international network of intellectuals and educators. The idea of an international commonwealth—establishing global harmony in a world of national sentiments—which attracted Smuts was consciously developed by Zimmern in his writings. Through them we can trace the emergence of a moral discourse surrounding the League—and its successor, the United Nations—and put this back in its real historical context, that of the effort by anxious elites to shore up a liberal world order that would be compatible with empire and Anglo-American hegemony for decades to come.[1]

∾

If Rome provided the Victorians with a frank model for empire, the Greeks offered the idea of a commonwealth devoted to the pursuit and defense of freedom. The early twentieth century, with the British Empire in flux after the Boer War, saw interest in the ancient Greeks become intense, and a flurry of popularizing works endeavored to explain their enduring value. Richard Livingstone published *The Greek Genius and Its Meaning to Us*; the historian Lowes Dickinson wrote his influential *The Greek View of Life*; and across the Atlantic, the Lowell Lectures for 1909 were given by the Hellenist John Mahaffy under the title *What Have the Greeks Done for Modern Civilization?* Among the more politically oriented of these works—and rather advanced in the attention it gave to economics and psychology—was *The Greek Commonwealth*, a study of Athens in the fifth century BC. Its author, Alfred Zimmern, was a thirty-two year old classicist and sociologist. Born in suburban Surrey into a cosmopolitan upper-middle-class family (Huguenot on one side, German-Jewish on the other), Zimmern was schooled at Winchester, read classics at the Hellenizing hothouse of New College, Oxford, and lectured there before quitting to travel around Greece itself for a year. Zimmern's study of the society and economy of fifth-century BC Athens was both a synthesis of recent scholarship and—at least in embryo—a political manifesto for the importance of Mind, liberty, and order. The Greeks, as he wrote, "are associated in our minds with a host of inherited ideas, with Art and Freedom, and Law and Empire. . . . [They were] the first and most congenial home of our distinctively Western civilization." The Greeks were, in Nietzsche's words (which Zimmern cited), "immortal teachers"; Zimmern's goal was to draw out the lessons and these he did in a fashion that made the moral basis of British global leadership unmistakably clear.[2]

The rise of Athens he portrayed as an unambiguous blessing for her neighbors. But it was not so much a triumph for reason (which was how it had been portrayed by earlier Victorians) as for the right kind of political and moral sentiments. Following Aristotle, he described the city-state as a model of political community because it encouraged real sociability based on common "primaeval emotions" of loyalty to friends and family: it was the closest man had come to the ideal of "the perfect citizen in the perfect state." It offered freedom because freedom was only possible in a justly ruled polity. If the Athenians had, as he wrote, a healthy skepticism about "the capacity of Parliaments," that was all to the good, because the polity was properly governed by enlightened and efficient men. Just like the British, the Athenian navy patrolled the seas, sent out colonists to form autonomous city-states elsewhere, and promoted commerce. The city's beneficial influence even extended beyond the borders of what Zimmern sometimes called its empire and sometimes the commonwealth: "For this also was part of the imperial mission—to give of their best to men and nations. . . . Athens could no more step back than most Englishmen feel they can leave India." Indeed the period following the peace with the Persians was, in his words, "perhaps the greatest and happiest period in recorded history" and in a Thucydidean peroration, Zimmern explained how he thought the Athenians might have expressed their right to lead:

> We are the leaders of civilization, the pioneers of the human race. Our society and intercourse is the highest blessing man can confer. . . . We have found out the secret of human power, which is the secret of happiness. . . . The name we know it by is Freedom, for it has taught us that to serve is to be free. Do you wonder why it is that "Alone among Mankind" (will there ever be another nation which can understand what we mean?) we confer our benefits, not on calculation of self-interest, but in the fearless confidence of Freedom.[3]

Contemporary reviewers were struck by the idealism of Zimmern's portrayal, in particular his idea that the Athenian empire stood for freedom based on an innate sense of disinterested virtue expressed in the rule of law. Whether it had been quite so obsessed by freedom as he suggested was after all open to question. What about slavery, whose economic importance Zimmern notably downplayed? And if the Athenians were as noble and magnificent in character as he implied, how could they, within a few decades, have overreached themselves in the Peloponnesian Wars and committed the outrages and massacres that followed?

But this idealism was entirely characteristic of his age and milieu. At Oxford, in the second half of the nineteenth century, a powerful school of liberal neo-Hegelians had emerged around the figure of a charismatic don called Thomas Hill Green. Green, and those he taught and inspired—who included a goodly proportion of the empire's governing class at the end of the century—found in German thought an intensely ethical and communitarian alternative to the prevailing philosophy of liberal self-interest and utilitarian calculation. Green and his students transformed the meaning of freedom and emphasized the importance of communal awareness in producing the good citizen. Ethics, they taught, could not be separated from politics. The free individual was the one who found self-realization from a sense of moral responsibility toward the community of which he formed a part. Reading a weakened version of evangelical Christianity and a powerful strain of Kant back into Aristotle's *Ethics*, they found in the Greek texts an eternal ideal of sociable selflessness, a political system driven toward perfection by an ethics of mutual assistance. The mechanics of government, the precise composition of the laws, did not concern them; it was men's minds that ultimately effected change—men driven not by vanity or self-interest but on the contrary by the Aristotelian and Stoic ideals of moderation, self-development, and the ability to rise above petty sectional interest to see the Good of the Whole. They were Hegelians insofar as they believed in the rationality of the historical process, and their place in its vanguard, although unlike

Hegel they did not place all their trust in state power because they believed that force could never substitute for willed engagement. They fused Hegel and Aristotle in seeing change as a progressive unfolding of man's capacity for self-realization. Above all, they were Kantians, with Kant's tight interconnection between reason, virtue, and freedom.[4]

Although the internationalist implications of this approach were rarely spelled out they could be glimpsed in embryo already in Green's own work. Just as for individuals, so for communities and nations was self-determination—meaning lack of external compulsion—the basis for freedom, and such freedom was only conducive to moral perfection when used in the consciousness of a dedication to others. If nationalism was something akin to a natural sense of community, the only practicable internationalism was one which recognized the necessity—not perhaps for states in the strict sense—but for nations, and which created the possibility for their cooperation. This, then, was not a form of cosmopolitanism in which national allegiances would be overridden in the name of a single community of world citizens, but much as for Smuts, a global order which worked through and encompassed the natural communitarian sentiment that was nationalism. But that greater order *would* inevitably evolve: Green himself fantasized about the emergence of "an international court with authority resting on the consent of independent states" and saw "every advance in the organization of mankind in states" as tending toward the emergence of such international organizations.[5]

Green died in 1882, the year that the British occupation of Egypt signaled the onset of a new frenetic phase of European colonial expansion. The resulting Scramble for Africa posed a challenge to his creed of disinterested benevolence and made empire look an altogether dirtier and less noble business. Yet his message of enlightened statesmanship survived and was even reinforced. It was about the time that Zimmern went up to Oxford that the Boer War galvanized J. A. Hobson into penning his well-known critique of the phenomenon of imperialism. Although it is remembered today chiefly for its economistic analysis of the causes of the European landgrab, Hobson's work was equally remarkable for its ambivalent stance on the broader question of empire. Hobson ridiculed the idea that any nation could be trusted to act as a civilizing influence abroad. But he recognized that the power of the West over the rest of the world was too great to be resisted, and he took it for granted that "civilized white nations" might legitimately control the affairs of "lower races." What he regarded as really pernicious—and the cause of the Boer War—was the unregulated greed—finance imperialism—that triumphed when foreign policy was subordinated to private enterprise and the pursuit of profit. The crux of the problem, for Hobson as it was for Smuts, Woodrow Wilson, and so many others of their generation, was ethical: mankind needed to be guided by altruism not selfishness. The solution, in Hobson's words, was to guide "scientific statecraft" so that "this process of development may ... yield a gain to world-civilization, instead of some terrible *debacle* in which revolted slave races may trample down their parasitic and degenerate white masters." Philosophically, he argued that the "principle of social utility" should be expanded internationally in order to define "the good of humanity." And his practical solution was confident of the merits of public governance: a genuinely impartial international body that might monitor the behavior of Western colonists.[6]

Similar feelings animated Zimmern's mentor, Gilbert Murray, the Australian-born classicist who became an even more ardent supporter of the League than Zimmern himself. In a 1900 essay, "The Exploitation of Inferior Races in Ancient and Modern Times," Murray tried— "in a purely scientific spirit"—to solve what he called the "Imperial labour problem" posed by the growth of white man's rule over "coloured men." "Those whom we cannot utilize we exterminate," Murray wrote, alluding critically to his experiences in Australia. "Those whom we can utilize we protect and often enable to increase in numbers." In his view, the spread of white power around the world was inexorable and so too therefore the subjugation of weaker peoples. The best that could be hoped for was protection of the latter through impartial imperial administrators, ruling through law.[7]

The young Zimmern himself deplored the contamination of the idea of empire by self-interested lobby groups, adventurers, and profiteers, but he had less confidence than Hobson in the possibilities of "scientific statecraft" and more in the high moral ideals embedded in the classics and their diffusion. When it appeared in 1911, *The Greek Commonwealth* brought Green's idealism into the ancient Athenian polity, and by Hellenizing many familiar older tropes about the virtues of British rule, and combining them with the most modern approaches to political psychology, presented it as an exemplary empire of freedom. The very title of Zimmern's book was deliberately chosen. He formed part of a circle known as the Round Table, an astonishingly influential study group of young men dedicated to thinking through the relationship between the Dominions and Britain, and much interested in the question of international commonwealth. Populated mostly by Oxford idealists mentored by South Africa High Commissioner Lord Milner, the Round Table had been searching since the Boer War to find a solution to what they regarded as the most pressing international problem of the day—how to reconcile the growing nationalism evident in the white settler colonies of the British Empire with continued rule from London. Australia, Canada, New Zealand and— since 1910—the Union of South Africa (not to mention Ireland) were all demanding greater political rights. *The Greek Commonwealth* alluded unmistakably to these contemporary preoccupations: "commonwealth" along Athenian lines would allow some degree of autonomy to the colonies—or to some of them—while preserving and justifying continued governance (and protection) from London.[8]

Zimmern's book was much discussed by these commonwealth theorists. They too felt that the empire, properly guided, could come close "to that union of all mankind of which some idealists have dreamed."[9] It is worth noting that the great advantage of the British Commonwealth/Empire, for Zimmern, was its flexibility.

It could evolve and accommodate others' political aspirations precisely because it lacked any definite centralized state or a clear constitutional system: it was all the stronger for having come into existence through the emergence of a shared consciousness rather than as a result of a political machinery. Like all enduring polities, it was essentially a social organism unified by a common moral purpose and culture: these were what secured its unity. Already one could see embryonically the split between the idealists like Zimmern and Murray and the sociologically inclined thinkers such as Hobson or Leonard Woolf: for the former, international *organizations*—however badly needed—were not in themselves the answer to the problem of world order; they could not survive unless behind them there occurred a deeper transformation in people's thinking, unless they fostered the organic emergence of a new consciousness of the ties that bound people of different nations, a new sense of global community. If they worked, they would work slowly, and need time. [10]

And one could also see, in this insistent focus on the settler colonies, a reluctance to face up fully to the unpalatable fact—which Hobson had pointed out—that the New Imperialism of the 1880s had brought large parts of the world under European sway in which settlers, if they existed at all, formed a tiny minority and where economic exploitation of local commodities and labor was the basic rationale for possession. Ancient Greek colonization—and indeed ancient Greek values—might seem to provide a template for Britain's relations with New Zealand or Canada (provided one did not dwell on the fate of their indigenous populations), but it was hardly applicable to the situation of India or the African colonies.[11]

During the First World War, Zimmern and other members of the Round Table entered wartime government service. As they began the intense discussions that were their contribution to the establishment of the League of Nations, it was this idea of commonwealth that shaped their thoughts. Commonwealth, after all, suggested that national and international organizations were not mutually incompatible, that on the contrary, they could be mutually reinforcing. Commonwealth, wrote Round Table ideologue Lionel Curtis, in his exhaustive wartime study *The Problem of the Commonwealth*, also involved "a special obligation to serve" backward races as they were ushered—eventually—into the realm of civilization. Because Zimmern in particular believed that what counted was national sentiment rather than state sovereignty, he liked the idea of the British Empire as a model for organizations in which less powerful nations, with or without (in the case of more primitive peoples) some kind of state of their own enjoyed the benefits of association with a larger power and the energies of individual countries could ultimately be reconciled within a universal world Whole. As he put it near the end of the war, both German militarism and Russian Bolshevism had to be opposed by a nobler ideal for humanity—"the principle of the Commonwealth."[12]

This faith in the commonwealth idea—which for some Round Table participants verged on the mystical—was tempered by the First World War into something considerably more practical. But in its basic presuppositions it was easily accommodated to the equally lofty worldview of the American president Woodrow Wilson. Wilson's long-standing notion of a "community of power" based on organic societies shared a similar faith in the basically corporate character of nations and a similar dislike of the self-centeredness of more individualist strands of liberalism. For Woodrow Wilson, too, democracy and freedom were valuable because of the way they allowed citizens to see themselves as parts of a larger whole. (In Wilson's words, modern democracy was not about the rule of the many but about the rule "of the whole.")[13]

At this time, as we have already suggested, Smuts and Whitehall had a more profound impact on the shaping of the details of the League of Nations than either President Woodrow Wilson or the leading American internationalist circles. After all, Wilson came fairly late to the project in a concrete sense; during the war itself he frowned on discussion about the shape of a postwar world organization, and he ultimately disregarded both the radical and the legalist versions of the League that had dominated American public debate before 1918. Instead what to all intents and purposes he adopted and modified was a composite British draft that had been crafted in Whitehall over the previous three years. Smuts played the key role in publicizing the general idea. But it was the young Alfred Zimmern who had done much of the detailed drafting. One of the founders of the new League of Nations Society in 1917, he was put in charge the following year of the section of the Foreign Office commissioned to think through the international organization of the peace.[14]

Zimmern himself was later to summarize the enormous variety of unofficial schemes that emerged on the Entente side during the war. Most were chiefly concerned with the codification of international law, with creating safeguards against war, and with establishing mechanisms for conciliation and arbitration among members. They were shy of giving any future international organization too much power or permanence, of allowing it to do much beyond the settlement of international disputes, or of opening it to universal membership. Some saw the future in an expansion of the legalism that had produced the Hague Conventions; others in the technical approach behind the Universal Postal Union and similar specialized socioeconomic agencies. In neither case, did they seem to appreciate what was involved in moving to the idea of a general international agency that would take on some of the core functions of the modern sovereign state. For Zimmern, what was needed was neither "a lawyer's pipe-dream" (his veiled critique of the legalists) nor "slipping furtively into the world-community" through "gas and water internationalism" (the allusion here was to Woolf's Fabian Society blueprint), but rather an organization that would build on, and foster, the embryonic sense of world citizenship. Describing what he had in mind, Zimmern once again returned to "ancient Athens, the community to which the Western world owes the twin conceptions of Liberty and Law" and "to the moment in Athenian history corresponding to that in which the civilized

world finds itself today." What the world cried out for
was a law-maker who understood the importance of
sentiment, just as Solon had turned Athenians into citizens and made them all "jealous for the maintenance of
justice. "[15]

And for a brief moment in 1918, Zimmern had been
able to play the part—if not of Solon, then at least of
his draftsman. As head of the unit dealing with the
question of the League inside the Foreign Office, he
took an earlier draft for a postwar League of Nations
and transformed it, calling for a regular conference system (based on the idea of the wartime British Imperial
Conference) with a standing secretariat and with aspirations to universal membership. There would be space
for the international lawyers, the diplomats, and the
technicians, but all would find themselves coordinated
by a secretariat that, in Zimmern's words, would "be a
kind of central watch-tower for every kind of official
international cooperation" and would encourage the
further study of international problems.

In one area in particular, Zimmern took issue sharply
with the Americans. Woodrow Wilson was demanding
that the new organization "guarantee" national boundaries and stressing the emancipatory importance of the
idea of national self-determination. Zimmern felt this
was politically naive. Thanks to colleagues like the historians Louis Namier, Arnold Toynbee, and Robert
Seton-Watson, working alongside him in the FO's Political Intelligence Department, Zimmern was much more
aware than the Americans advising Wilson of the enormous ethnographic complexity of Eastern Europe. In

wartime talks and papers, he cautioned against the idea that a world of nation-states would bring peace, and he warned against fixing state boundaries too rigidly in parts of the world where "the sentiment of nationality is still undeveloped." Even where the sentiment existed, making it the basis of political organization was a recipe for disaster, he noted, alluding to southeastern Europe's travails. His paper raised the thorny question of minority rights but warned against making the League responsible for protecting minorities or for otherwise intervening in states' internal affairs.[16]

If nationalism in Eastern Europe he regarded as still evolving, in Africa Zimmern saw no signs of it at all. Like Smuts (who was much influenced by Zimmern's overall approach), he talked about trusteeships and the moral responsibility of civilized states toward backward peoples. Unlike Smuts, he believed supervision of tropical Africa in particular should be entrusted to a multinational commission capable of thinking in terms of "internationalism . . . which may be defined as the habit of looking at [a] problem from the point of view of the world as a whole." This was rather close to the idea that Hobson and other radical internationalists of the British Left had been advancing since the start of the century and it was here that Smuts—like other nationalists from the colonies—departed most decisively from the Zimmern draft. At Paris, they cast doubt on the practicability of an international administration of "more backward peoples" and hoped to exclude Germany's Pacific and African colonies entirely from the new mandate system on the grounds that they were "inhabited by barbarians who not only cannot possibly govern themselves but to whom it would be impracticable to apply any idea of self-determination in the European sense."[17]

This was a fundamental disagreement of the utmost importance for the future: could the most backward peoples of the world be prepared for national consciousness or not? At Paris negotiators left the question hanging while preserving international oversight for the foreseeable future. At one extreme, there was Smuts, who had his doubts. At the other there were the Americans who possessed—in the words of one British observer—"a childlike faith in the virtues of democracy." Zimmern believed in the educative function of "civilised control." Yet for almost everyone concerned, in Western capitals at least, this was basically a long-term problem and the mandate concept allowed them to fudge the issue.[18]

Where Zimmern and Smuts saw entirely eye to eye was over the need to make the new world organization a reality. Both agreed that one had to steer a midcourse between two extremes—on the one hand, the radical suggestion that had become quite popular during the war itself, that nation-states should be replaced by a democratic powerful World-State (something Zimmern regarded with horror), and on the other, the far more cautious approach of conservatives that the empire should be unencumbered by any new responsibilities, bar those of having to meet occasionally in concert with other great powers, much as had happened after Napoleon's defeat in 1815. Like Smuts, Zimmern rejected both. He hated the idea of a powerful World-State that was being called for by figures like H. G. Wells: in his view this was too mechanistic and impractical and it could only threaten repression, whereas a genuine international community required individuals to feel a sense of common moral purpose. But he also detested the idea of a very loose and informal Concert, since this went against the idea that human society could progress beyond the national and implied a pessimism about international affairs that, despite the war, he did not share: there was fundamentally no reason why, under the right guidance, people everywhere should not get along. The old balance of power had to be replaced by something both more modern—because that would reflect the economic interdependence of the contemporary world—and more desirable.[19]

Hence what Zimmern proposed for the peace negotiators to consider was something more enduring than an occasional conference and considerably less than a World State. The League would have a formal and continuing presence but it would essentially be a forum for the powers, and they would continue to make major decisions with few, if any, formal obligations (certainly far fewer than Woodrow Wilson sought). It would provide the chance for "a meeting of Governments with Governments, each [Government] preserving its own independence and being responsible to its own people."[20] From the British perspective, meanwhile, the League had a more specific purpose as well—it would cement the empire's ties with the United States, something that the war had shown to be essential for the continued survival of the empire itself, and get the Americans in particular to share the "burden of world government" in the peace.[21] In other words, one could view the League through a universalist lens and believe that it would usher in a new global sense of community, or one could view it through an imperial lens, as the precondition for Britain's continued world leadership, now in partnership with the Americans.

For Zimmern, these two Leagues were one and the same. His view, after all, was that the British Commonwealth was "not an English, nor an Anglo-Saxon but a world experiment."[22] In other words, if one believed—as he did—that the British Empire was the Athens of its day, and that preserving—indeed extending its sway—was the way to bring freedom (in the *real* sense) to the world, then the League could in fact serve the causes of empire and the broader interests of humanity simultaneously. Sure of the moral righteousness of their cause, the British could no more abdicate their world role than could the citizens of Periclean Athens. Instead, by spreading the sway of their impartial rule they would accustom peoples who had been governed by self-interested despots to the rule of law, the benefits of free trade, and easy international exchange. For men like Zimmern, the extension of British influence after 1918 into new regions like the Middle East could not be regarded as imperialism because it was not self-interested or rapacious: thanks to the British and French mandates, monitored by the League's Permanent Mandates Commission, peoples who had languished under Ottoman rule would now be brought into the orbit of modern civilization. Thanks, too, to the League, the nations of Eastern

Europe could enjoy the privilege of ruling themselves, and if they had to accept League oversight—in the way they managed their minorities—that was simply because they were inexperienced in these things and needed the wise counsel of those more experienced in the arts of government. Hellenism, after all, taught that "barbarians" could be brought into the "polis" of civilized mankind by educating "peoples unused to power" and teaching them the "philosophic discipline" of politics. In this way, they would come to free themselves from chauvinism, and see that the real meaning of the "great universal conceptions of justice and liberty" were more than mere "emanations of local self-will."[23]

This then was what the League of Nations was emphatically *not*. It was not a world government in embryo. And it was not a machine for global democracy intended to bring political independence to the rest of the world, or to dismantle the European colonial empires. On the contrary, in the eyes of Whitehall, it was a means to preserve and indeed extend British influence, to cement its world leadership role with the United States, and simultaneously to create a new order in the most important part of the world for the British—Europe. Empire and freedom were not only compatible; the one was necessary for the progressive extension of the latter. In Zimmern's words from *The Greek Commonwealth*, "to serve is to be free."

The Senate's rejection of U.S. membership in the League of Nations came as a major blow to proponents of this strategy. But logically, in view of his confidence that the very conditions of the modern world were reinforcing the new internationalism he believed in, Zimmern did not initially worry. Europe, he wrote in 1922, was "in convalescence." It might need "a revaluation of our own western values ... a new impetus towards the unseen," but he was confident about the young men who had come through the war able to unmask the pretensions of their elders and demanding cooperation among nations. And, on the positive side, he welcomed the rise of independent new states "mainly on the British model," across the "mother continent." Their emergence, he believed, meant the end of nineteenth-century balance of power politics and "for the first time in modern European history made wholehearted cooperation between the European states a possible policy." It was a verdict that someone more knowledgeable about East European affairs in particular would surely have hesitated to make.[24]

Education as a process of spiritual transformation—the Hellenic influence evident here—was the key, in Zimmern's view, to the successful consolidation of the new international system: men had to be encouraged to see "the world as a whole." Solutions for peace lay not in getting organizational details right but in "a social education for the individual": the values of T. H. Green endured. The kaiser's Germany had offered a negative example of schooling because it had made pupils feel they owed their allegiance to the state rather than to each other and had inculcated pride in national cultural distinctiveness rather than in the universal values of civilized humanism: the result had been militarism and world war. Between the wars, Zimmern therefore left public service and resumed his career as a university teacher and educator. He held a professorship in international relations with the newly founded chair in Aberystwyth and was later he was elected the first Montagu Burton Professor in the same subject at Oxford. In between he lectured at Cornell and helped run the League's International Institute for Intellectual Cooperation in Paris.

His beloved Greeks still guided him. As he wrote in his inaugural Oxford lecture in 1931, the world faced a choice between "Hellenization" and "a return to the Dark Ages," between "attempting to civilize the barbarians and abandoning our own city," and the success of the League itself depended on such a mental and spiritual reorientation. It certainly did not depend on such technical matters as the articulation of international law, something Zimmern thought tended to artificiality and regarded with some suspicion. Indeed he decried suggestions that the League could safeguard world peace merely by promoting a unified and standardized global system of international law as "not merely premature but . . . grotesque and ridiculous."[25] Similarly, Zimmern regarded the question of the League's precise political status as completely secondary. Let the political scientists puzzle it out. "The attempt to find old-fashioned political labels to fit new and unprecedented political entities is as futile in the case of the League of Nations as in the parallel instance of the 'British Commonwealth' or 'Empire.'" If it was anything, it was "an instrument of cooperation." Startlingly, he described the "League" itself as a label that was, in itself, "politically impotent"; life would only be breathed into it by the will of the peoples who made up the member states.[26]

As such comments suggest, it is wrong to see internationalists like Zimmern as wholehearted in their support of the League of Nations or to miss the imperial dimension that always remained so important to them. In a 1926 series of lectures delivered at Columbia University, Zimmern made it clear that he still regarded not the League but the British Empire as the world's best hope. This was not—according to him—the first British Empire, which had ended when the American colonies broke away, nor the land-grabbing Second, which had supposedly collapsed along with its continental counterparts during the Great War, but what he called the "Third British Empire" that now revolved around his beloved conception—the Commonwealth. The new rights granted the British Dominions after the First World War suggested a degree of constitutional dynamism and flexibility that based itself—much to Zimmern's approval—not on law itself but on the appeal to shared cultural norms and, more inchoately (and less to his approval), to "British race sentiment."[27] This brandnew empire of the 1920s was a model for the world: it had outlasted the war because it contained a "spirit of liberty" and "free institutions" not found in its rivals. The ties that bound it together were "not material but spiritual," and "the tie of force" had been altered gradually into "a tie of passive acquiescence." The argument ignored India or the African colonies where even as he wrote, resistance to British rule was gathering. But Zimmern was convinced that moral rather than military or police power had kept the empire—the "largest single political community in the world"—together and turned it into "the surest bulwark against war in the present-day world."[28]

Depicted by him as a world community in the making, this culturally and racially diverse empire was made up of "a large variety of communities at a number of different stages in their advance towards complete self-government." (Japanese theorists of empire, as we shall see, agreed: the League of Nations was basically a European club; the British Empire provided the real model for a world community.) The war, fought in the name of freedom—according to Zimmern—had accelerated the empire's emancipatory dynamic. India, he noted with pleasure, despite lacking self-government, had been admitted to the League of Nations; the mandates had turned former colonial powers into trustees; and Egypt had moved in a few years from Ottoman province to British protectorate to independence. At the same time, the empire had come to appreciate the necessity for international cooperation through the League itself; indeed the latter, by bolstering the new international society of states "provides the outline at least of a system fitted to replace that which passed away for Britain in 1914." The League was thus the deus ex machina of the empire, and the latter's survival would require it to find a new place as "a league within the larger League, a society within that larger society."

But the League required the empire too, because as a newcomer it still lacked the "moral authority" the British Empire possessed. There was for Zimmern really only one area that threatened to gravely compromise this authority—the question of racial equality. Here was where Zimmern parted company from Smuts—reflecting a division within the ranks of British liberal thinking on empire that was to have significant repercussions in the future. Like Smuts, Zimmern felt that "the white man's prestige" had been weakened by the war and by the spread of scientific and technological knowledge. Unlike Smuts, he thought there was no stopping this process without losing the moral superiority that he always identified with the British. This was why in his view the principle of self-determination—something which characteristically he defined as "on its deeper side, a movement for the affirmation of human personality"—could not be held back from nonwhite peoples. Zimmern deplored the defeat at Paris in 1919 of the Japanese proposal to commit the League of Nations to racial equality, and he appealed to the "established British principle in regard to racial distinctions of . . . complete equality," looking forward to the day when an Indian government would, with British support, successfully reintroduce the Japanese initiative. The Smutsian alternative, which he ruled out, was to countenance permanent British imperial rule on the "basis of white supremacy." In this sense, he concluded, world peace rested on "the moral courage of Britain." Once again, world order and stable relations between peoples required moral leadership more than they did new institutions and laws.[29]

In its third edition by 1934, Zimmern's *The Third British Empire* was hailed by a reviewer in the liberal internationalists' house journal, *International Affairs*, as outlining "*the* great example of the sort of international cooperation on which a stable system of organized world relations can be erected," demonstrating that "no legal sanctions can be so efficient or permanent as the free and spontaneous willingness to cooperate which is the real foundation of the British Empire today."[30] Yet even if one accepted the deeply problematic picture of the empire painted by Zimmern—one which, as suggested above, skimmed implausibly over the sheer coercion required to keep it together—how could one be sure that the rest of the world would think about its future along the lines Zimmern approved? How, in *his* words, could one be sure that "the Continental and Asiatic people not to mention those of the two Americas, had simply been turned into Englishmen"?[31]

Zimmern himself could not but acknowledge that much of the world was not yet thinking internationally and needed help. Eventually, people everywhere would come to learn that war was irrational; meantime, educators could help the process along while rational statesmen and policymakers guarded the peace. International relations chairs and the International Institute for Intellectual Cooperation were not the only institutions founded between the wars to foster internationalism and a transvaluation of European values. Zimmern was also linked to the establishment of pioneering foreign policy think-tanks like the Institute for International Affairs in London and the Council on Foreign Relations in New York, sister-institutions designed explicitly to help cement Anglo-American world leadership. And he was in close touch with Wilsonians like Columbia University professor James Shotwell, who worked with him on the Institute for Intellectual Cooperation, thereby keeping an American toe in the League of Nations door.[32]

But as fascism spread, an economic slump undermined liberal capitalism, and Hitler came to power, pinning hopes of world peace on liberal education—whether based on the eternal values of the Greeks or the new discipline of international relations which would translate those values for the modern age—seemed a quixotic enterprise at best. The intellectuals in whom Zimmern had reposed such trust argued among themselves about pacifism. Some insisted that it was necessary to turn the League into an alliance of democracies with its own international police force to back it up. Others, like Zimmern, shuddered since this ran counter to his belief in reasonableness and the transformative power of the spirit. Yet his own Hellenization process had clearly failed. The rise of powerful and self-confident alternative militant ideologies on Left and Right revealed the practical limitations of his moral idealism and exposed its lack of cultural self-consciousness. T. H. Green's idealism might have served the imperial elites of the 1880s but "the principle of Commonwealth" offered no answer to Hitler or Stalin. Sounding like nothing so much as a disconsolate school headmaster, in 1938 Zimmern lamented the "decline in international standards" and admitted that none of the three forces he had anticipated would lead to improvement—Christianity, "our own English standard of behavior," and international law—had worked. He seemed shocked that states continued to pursue their own interests, that the "German mind" had not withstood the temptations of Nazism, and that international public opinion was failing to prevent the drift to war. His earlier interest in the social and economic dimensions of political life had apparently vanished; all that was left was a complaint at the collapse of international morality, completely divorced from any analysis of the balance of power or strategic interest.

It was at this time that the historian E. H. Carr—in a polemic that would have a considerable influence on the subsequent study of international relations—accused Zimmern (among others) of wishful thinking, a lack of realism, and failure to recognize the primacy of power in international affairs. Carr's *Twenty Years' Crisis* was praised and attacked in equal measure, and after the war, in particular, tough-minded theorists would echo its demolition of "idealism." Contemporaries were less bowled over: one critic astutely noted that although Carr seemed to regard morality as the opposite of power, he never really defined what he meant by the term; it was all very well to link morality with utopia, power with reality, but the consequence was to make it appear that moral values were somehow less real than power in shaping social reality. As for Zimmern, he stuck to his guns. Moral relativism was abhorrent to him. He believed that there was no advantage to be had in "running away from the notion of good . . . or by refusing to admit that one foreign policy or one national tradition or one political cause can be 'better' than another." Indeed what many critics, understandably, missed about his own works was that they were often written not so much as impartial assessments of the course of events as exhortations to moral and political improvement. [33]

The Second World War did however erode Zimmern's confidence in the possibility of European recovery and finally undermined something that had been even dearer to him—his faith in the British Empire. By the early 1940s, he had become convinced that the only hope for the future of the world lay in persuading the United States to play the leadership role that had previously been reserved for the British. He worked for a while on postwar planning in the wartime Foreign Office, and he was centrally involved in helping to set up the successor to the Institute for Intellectual Cooperation—UNESCO— before being replaced as its head by the British biologist Julian Huxley. (He and Huxley disagreed sharply about what intellectual cooperation meant in the circumstances of the mid-1940s. For Zimmern, it meant keeping alive the values of liberalism and supporting the "moral rearmament" of the West in defense of freedom. For Huxley this was both old-fashioned and unnecessarily combative: he advocated instead the dissemination of a scientific humanism that would bring people together across ideological boundaries on the basis of the objective truths of science.) In 1947, professionally disappointed, Zimmern left for the United States.[34]

He was moving to a country for which he had always had a high regard and in the year of the Truman Doctrine and the Marshall Plan, the sixty-eight-year-old Zimmern hailed the youthful superpower's emergence onto the world stage. An article of his entitled "Athens and America" highlighted the similarities between the ancient Greeks and the modern Americans—their "astounding vigour and freshness of mind," their ability to rejuvenate even "jaded and discouraged visitants from the Old World." Both welcomed the immigrant and had extraordinary powers of cultural assimilation; both too had an "expansive quality"—had not Alexander the Great benefited from the Macedonian phalanx ("the atomic bomb of its day") to spread the genius of Greek civilization? And just as Athens had combined the forces of the Greeks to defend civilization ("in the strict sense of that term") in the face of the Persian threat, so she offered a model of leadership for the federalists in Washington. Of course, the story could end badly: Zimmern recalled the Athenian hubris and the expedition to Melos, in which "on a miniature scale" they had behaved no better than Nazis. But the tenor of his argument was extraordinarily, even implausibly effusive: from the fifth century BC until the rise of the United States after 1945, he now claimed, "predominant power in world affairs was never in the hands of a people dedicated to the principles of constitutional democracy." In a subsequent book on *The American Road to World Peace*, he elaborated: the Roman Empire, it turned out, had been a corruption of Hellenic principles and its legacy had infected European history with illiberalism; American federalism was the true successor to Greek democracy and hence the world's best hope for preserving international peace. There was almost no mention of the British Empire, which Zimmern had believed in for more than half a century as a force for good. Zimmern now suggested that throughout the two millennia that separated Pericles from Harry Truman, the world had languished in utter darkness. Fortunately, the "European Age" had ended and the World Spirit had moved on, and it was now the United States of America not the British Commonwealth of Nations that held the best chance of making the Charter of the United Nations "as true a constitution for the whole of mankind as the laws of Athens were for Athenians." Only the United States, which had shown in its own history how the rule of law could be spread over a vast and diverse population through the inculcation of a dynamic sense of social morality, could plausibly enthrone Law and Liberty across the globe.[35]

⌐∽

Zimmern's reputation among American political scientists was considerable at this time but his reading of their country's constitutional development struck them as ignorant and optimistic. More fundamentally, his entire approach to international affairs came under challenge as commentators and intellectuals debated the meaning of America's rise to world power. Even before it reinvented itself as Cold War social "science," taking it ever further away from Zimmern's legacy, the discipline of international relations in the 1950s came under the spell of realism, a doctrine that put power and force firmly back in the center of the picture and prided itself on its tough-minded ethics of self-interest. In 1951, the most influential figure in the field in the United States, Hans Morgenthau, launched a blistering attack on the utopian strand of thought in American foreign policy, which had led first Woodrow Wilson and then Roosevelt and Truman to jeopardize the national interest by their high-minded but naïve internationalism. Now there was a new reading of the Greeks—only neither Aristotle nor Plato but Thucydides provided the inspiration. International politics were a matter of tragic conflict and competition not the mutually beneficial pursuit of the good life. Each state fought for what it could get; cooperation was impossible except on the basis of common interests, an approach Zimmern had always disliked. He believed, he would say, in responsibility politics not power politics, in morality as an essential element of world affairs.[36]

Well before the Second World War, the idea that the world was converging on the values of a single international civilization—rooted in the classics but exemplified by European, and preferably Victorian British norms— was starting to look willfully self-congratulatory. What European civilization could conceivably encompass Britain, France, Nazi Germany, Fascist Italy, and the USSR? In 1929, Sir John Fischer Williams confessed that the "concept of "civilized society" as a community of nations or states distinct from the rest of the world no longer corresponds with the main facts of contemporary life." The interwar crisis of democracy in Europe accelerated this erosion of confidence. By the 1940s, the liberal landscape was split between those, like world historian Arnold Toynbee, who acknowledged that the Victorian path to universalism was blocked off, and those who sought to resuscitate it through notions of the West or

American exceptionalism. Preeminent among the latter were the Cold War Atlanticists, of whom Zimmern was now one, who saw in the concept of "Western" civilization, a new receptacle for perennial truths and a way of passing the torch of world leadership on to their American charges. In the early Cold War, British foreign secretary Ernest Bevin recommended "the spiritual consolidation of western civilisation" to U.S. secretary of state George Marshall while British historian Sir Edward Woodward lectured American students on "the heritage of Western civilization" and warned them that America would have to step in and save Europe for the sake of the "good life" of the entire world. For his part, Toynbee worried that such talk heralded the onset of "a coming American world empire."[37]

Zimmern himself would certainly not have shared Toynbee's misgivings. He hoped that American support would make the United Nations a success, and he had some reason for optimism. Public enthusiasm for the new world body was high after the war in the United States, and former students of his were rising to prominence in the Truman administration. One of these, Dean Rusk, headed the State Department's Office of UN Affairs from where he tried to turn the UN General Assembly into a pro-American tool that could bypass the Soviet veto. Zimmern was supportive, urging Rusk in 1947 to push an "American Programme" through the UN. But Rusk cautioned his former teacher against expecting too much: he himself was disappointed that neither the Truman Doctrine nor the Marshall Plan assigned any role to the United Nations but gradually came to accept that the structure of the UN meant it would remain generally a secondary forum for the pursuit of American interests.[38]

Briefly, when the Soviet Union withdrew temporarily from the Security Council over China, Rusk was indeed able to use the United Nations in the way he and Zimmern envisaged. In June 1950 it was Rusk who was instrumental in taking advantage of the Soviet absence from the Security Council to get the council's backing for action in Korea, drafting a resolution— "Uniting for Peace"—around a creative misreading of the Charter in order to shift the initiative to the General Assembly. It was an action that demonstrated a Zimmernlike willingness to deploy the new world body in pursuit of the defense of freedom as defined by the United States. Zimmern himself argued at this time that the Security Council had become a stumbling block to international action and approved both of the turn to the General Assembly and the rise of regional collective security alliances. But by the mid-1950s, it was clear that the U.S. flirtation with the UN was basically over. Rusk's belief that "humanitarian diplomacy" was part of America's world mission, that it was for the United States to "take a lead in raising the moral standards of international society," and that an effective United Nations was needed for this purpose, all echoed long-standing beliefs of Zimmern himself. Nevertheless, faced with a divergence between the goals of the world hegemon and the world body, both men unhesitatingly opted for the former. What mattered was educating the world in the values of freedom, not supporting the UN per se.[39]

The spread of morality, at least as Zimmern defined it, demanded world leadership, and this was something that fell to the United States, not to the UN, to provide. It was the United States, not the UN, that must lead "international society" through the "beneficial use of power" and through its "civilising influence." What would happen if the United States ceased to cultivate the UN in the ways of "responsibility politics" and the "extension of the realm of Law" was not something Zimmern addressed. The most he would concede was that the rest of the world had difficulty realizing that the United States was not a traditional great power— that "there are still many nations, particularly nonwhite nations, who have not yet brought themselves to trust the American government and people or to recognize that the central place on the political stage of the world is now occupied by a Great Power of a type very different from that of its European predecessors, and representing new principles and new standards of conduct in international relationships."[40]

Zimmern's ideas may seem Victorian, his belief in the expertise and far-sightedness of statesmen and policymakers old-fashioned. And one might question whether one can have his sense of moral community on a global scale without the rest of the conceptual baggage that accompanied it—the belief in a single (Western) civilization, the Hegelian need and praise for a world leader, the ethical conception of the state, and the reluctance to entertain any element of moral relativism. Nevertheless, many commentators even today seem to like the idea of an "international society" (a term which he may have originated) linked not by formal norms, still less by international organizations with their cumbersome and self-serving bureaucracies but rather by a shared sense of moral community. And there are many—in the United States in particular—who still live in Zimmern's shadow in a much closer sense. Like Zimmern, they believe that the world leader can never be *primarily* actuated by self-interest: it acts for the best and its motives cannot be questioned even if its performance can. Across the political spectrum, they believe that the world needs a leader and that this can only be the United States. Former secretary of state Madeleine Albright once talked notoriously about the United States as the "indispensable nation." Fareed Zakaria describes U.S. power as "not merely good for America [but] good for the world."[41] James Traub's *The Freedom Agenda*, unsparingly analyses the failures of the Bush administration's neo-Wilsonianism, only to conclude that it was only the execution not the basic idea that was flawed. And in *Forging a World of Liberty under Law*—a set of 2006 proposals for rethinking American national security—Princeton political scientists see the United States, much as Zimmern had seen the British Empire, as *the* force for good in an increasingly interconnected world. They too speak the language of expanding freedom and regard the triumph of their values—which conveniently happen to be both American *and* universal—as all but inevitable. Just as Zimmern had talked about empire in terms of commonwealth, downplaying its coercive and violent underpinnings, so they talk about America's "edge" in the "networked century" and define the new measure of power as "connectedness." Ironically, this brings them very close to the neo-Marxist vision of twenty-first-century empire popularized by Hardt and Negri, though they refrain pointedly from acknowledging any element of domination in this scenario. How, after all, can there be coercion in the empire of freedom? One might have thought that the events of the twentieth and early twenty-first centuries would make it hard to take the idea of the virtuous hegemon seriously, and hard too to assume that the most powerful state in the world will be best placed to define the common purpose. Yet it seems not to be so: the question of who should decide what is good for the world seems to remain as self-evident to today's international moralists as it did a century ago to Zimmern himself. [42]

3

Chapter

§

Nations, Refugees, and Territory

THE JEWS AND THE LESSONS OF THE NAZI NEW ORDER

For imperial internationalists like Smuts or Zimmern, the struggle with fascism did not fundamentally alter the arguments they had long advanced for a commonwealth of nations. There were lessons to be learned, to be sure, from the League's collapse—above all the need to make sure that the great powers were united within whatever organization replaced it. But in essence they regarded the new United Nations Organization as similar in its goals to its predecessor. It was to be a device for cushioning the British Empire, cementing its ties with the United States, and coming to terms with the unfortunate but tolerable fact that the Soviet Union had become a world power. By keeping the peace, it would preserve the global hegemony of Europe and its successor states.

These were the nations that mattered, those that in Zimmern's words understood the "philosophical discipline" of politics—or were supposed to. The 1919 settlement had barred the principle of national self-determination from Africa and Southeast Asia but extended it across Central and Eastern Europe. And it was there—in Europe's borderlands—that interwar border disputes and angry minorities raised *the* central question of world order—how to achieve international harmony in a system of nation-states. If mutually recognizing nation-states were to constitute the basic building blocks of the future international system, how could tensions between them—tensions that seemed hardwired into the prewar and interwar European state system—be prevented from erupting time after time into war?

As many in Whitehall had feared all along, the triumph of national self-determination after 1918 had simply replaced one problem with another. Smuts, Wilson, and Zimmern all (with differing degrees of enthusiasm) had hailed the extension of the principle of national autonomy, but they quickly realized that what they were now faced with was something new—preventing minorities from becoming a major source of international conflict. This was perhaps *the* single most important challenge to interwar diplomacy in the Old Continent, and it was one the League had signally failed to solve. Its pioneering legal mechanisms for ensuring that minorities were properly treated never worked because the great powers were never prepared to insist that their East European allies respect them.

With ethnic Germans the largest single minority in the region, the inadequacy of the minority rights system provoked growing dissatisfaction in Berlin. After 1933, Nazism became the self-proclaimed alternative to the League—a movement dedicated to using force where law had failed to protect Germans abroad, and beyond that to eradicate minorities completely by redrawing

East European boundaries through war and violent population politics. Nazism's rise demonstrated nationalism's potential to expel unwanted peoples en masse, creating massively destabilizing flows of refugees and raising tensions across the European continent and beyond.

At the center of the Nazi vision of Europe was, of course, the elimination of Jewish life on the continent. Inevitably, therefore, it was around the Jewish question that these broader issues of nationality, statelessness and minority rights crystallized. With the British paralyzed on the question because of their role as mandatory power in Palestine, it fell to the United States to push for a more energetic global response to the refugee crisis. This chapter explores how wartime analysts of Nazi rule in Europe shaped their prescriptions for the future of minority rights, national self-determination, and refugee welfare on the basis of their interpretations of what was happening during the war itself. In particular, as the Final Solution unfolded, commentators and activists in the United States argued about how Europe's postwar Jewish question should be tackled by the allied United Nations. Diametrically opposed views could be, and were, derived from the study of what the Nazis were doing. Some experts remained committed to versions of the old idea of minority rights protection and still placed their faith in international legal safeguards; indeed they now proposed expanding and even universalizing these far beyond Eastern Europe. But others saw that the world order for which the United Nations were fighting differed from its predecessor precisely in

its more sober assessment of what international law
could actually achieve. Indeed more and more went to
the opposite extreme: for them, the lesson of the Nazi
New Order was that eliminating minorities was simply
a necessary part of modern nationalism and modern internationalism alike; what was desirable therefore was
to rationalize forced population transfers and exchanges
by making sure they were internationally negotiated
and organized rather than spontaneous and disorgan-
ized outcomes of war or unilateral fiat. Would the postwar order support the hopes of the believers in international law, or the proponents of ethical homogeneity?

৬৯

Europe's Jewish question had figured centrally in international thinking about national and minority rights
since the end of the nineteenth century. At the framing
of the peace in 1919, it was one of the key issues that
tied the League of Nations to the terms of the postwar
settlement after Jewish lobbyists at Versailles succeeded
in having international recognition of the new states of
Eastern Europe made dependent on their observation of
minority rights guaranteed by League of Nations oversight. East European delegates in Paris publicly protested at the humiliation of being forced to report to an
international body on how they treated their own citizens, but their position was undercut by reports of pogroms in eastern Poland, Romania, and the Ukraine.
What started out as a discussion of "national rights" for
Jews turned into a more sweeping system of protecting

minorities everywhere from the Baltic states to the Aegean, as well as in parts of the Middle East. A small secretariat at the League headquarters in Geneva received complaints of minorities' ill-treatment and could investigate and report on what they found. As with the League's oversight of mandates, minority rights, though guaranteed in law, were essentially to be protected by the force of international public opinion. Still, they represented the most intrusive intervention by international law yet sanctioned in the domestic affairs of sovereign states—so intrusive that the great powers ruled out applying the same kind of regime to themselves.[1]

By the mid-1930s the League minority rights regime was in disarray. The degree of intervention implied in the domestic affairs of East European states was bitterly resented; yet the League's architects had failed to provide for any enforcement mechanisms, thereby alienating minority groups as well and the powers that sometimes backed them. Moreover, because Germany, as a great power, had not been subjected to such oversight, there was virtually no legal basis for Geneva to intervene after the Nazis began to target the Jews inside the Reich. Once the League's prestige waned, East European states—starting with Poland—ceased to bother with their formal obligations either toward their minorities, and in fact began to follow Germany in implementing boycotts, the numerus clausus, and other similar discriminatory policies, in an obvious effort to reduce Jews in particular to second-class status and to encourage them to leave. By 1937, Europe was facing a refugee crisis of proportions unparalleled since the end of the Great War.

The League of Nations seemed powerless to help. There was no general definition of who counted as a refugee, and indeed hundreds of thousands of stateless persons had been living in legal limbo for two decades. Fridtjof Nansen, who held the position of high commissioner for refugees in the 1920s, gave the issue publicity, but his office lacked authority; after his death in 1930, it was downgraded. In 1933, a convention helped regulate the plight of many Russian, Armenian, Assyrian, and other refugees, but no sooner had this been achieved than the Nazis came into power. The League established a special office to deal with refugees from the Third Reich, but other countries, with high numbers of their own citizens unemployed, were extremely reluctant to admit them. James MacDonald, the League's high commissioner for refugees from Germany resigned in frustration in 1935: his call for the Nazi regime to be replaced was ignored.[2]

The global refugee crisis testified to the League's failure and threatened to plunge Europe into another war. Hitler argued that Germany was overcrowded, that surplus populations of inferior racial stock had to be jettisoned, and that the Germans themselves—deprived in 1918 of their prewar colonies overseas as well as of chunks of the prewar Reich—needed more land. Yet this argument was not only to be found among Nazis. There was, in fact, general agreement that Europe was suffering from a chronic problem of overpopulation, that it needed to be able to export its surplus populations overseas, and that post-1918 barriers to migration flows had contributed to worsening international tension. Agricultural economists pointed to chronic underemployment in the agrarian states of Eastern and Southern Europe; fascist demographers argued that colonization in North and East Africa would help solve the problem, at least in Italy.

The issue certainly did not go unobserved in Washington, where President Roosevelt was concerned both about the specific plight of Jewish refugees and about Europe's broader demographic crisis. Here was one area where he seized the opportunity early on to try to assert American leadership internationally. He was keenly aware of the difficulty that had been caused by the U.S. immigration restrictions in the early 1920s, and he saw the problem in global terms. He commissioned geographers to find scientific solutions—solutions that would simultaneously pacify Europe and promote economic development and civilization in the rest of the world through organized colonization and settlement. What was needed—in his view—was not merely to find homes for those who needed them, but to broker international agreements between "refugee exporting countries" and potential recipients. The abortive international refugee conference held at Evian in France in July 1938 was intended not only to channel aid quickly to German and Austrian refugees, but in the longer-term to lead to the establishment of an international machinery for finding homes for Europe's surplus population. But the Intergovernmental Committee, established to supervise "orderly emigration" and to develop opportunities for "permanent settlement" not only failed on its own terms; its very existence, outside the formal structures of the League of Nations, pointed to the League's own failure to grapple with the problem.[3]

Despite this, Roosevelt persevered. A Wilsonian for a new generation, he was convinced that his predecessor had failed to build a lasting peace because he had ignored the powerful social forces generated by the impact of modern politics on populations. If the failed Versailles order had been the work of a generation of Oxbridge classicists, perhaps now American social science, as handmaiden to enlightened statesmanship, could take over and help find a solution to the European Malthusian nightmare. "Tremendously interested" in the subject already by late 1938, Roosevelt had responded to Kristallnacht by asking his favorite geographer, Johns Hopkins president Isaiah Bowman, to recommend resettlement options for Jews worldwide. "Frankly," he had told him. "What I am looking for is the possibility of uninhabited or sparsely inhabited good agricultural lands to which Jewish colonies might be sent." Venezuela, Colombia? Bowman responded by warning that the possibilities were limited, but identified places in Central and South America, though the settlers would "have to bring their culture with them."[4]

Such was the thinking behind the top-secret so-called M-Project (M for Migration) which emerged in Washington during the war. Through Bowman, Roosevelt brought in teams of geographers and anthropologists, led by M-Project head, Henry Field, who commissioned a huge series of studies on migration and settlement "since population pressures had often caused wars throughout history." Somewhere in Roosevelt's quicksilver mind the fate

of the Jews, peace in Europe, and the development of
the Middle East were interconnected. Even before setting up the M-Project, he had talked secretly with advis-
ers about joining with Britain and France in financing
"an Arab transfer to Iraq." Once the war broke out,
such plans took second place to keeping Britain afloat
and defeating Germany. Nevertheless, his first question
to Field was for an estimate of the maximum population
of Iraq "provided water control of the Tigris and
Euphrates is re-established with irrigation projects and
barrages, agricultural development and improved public
health measures." But the remit of the operation ran far
wider than the Middle East. By 1942, M-Project per-
sonnel were covering global manpower and settlement
possibilities in enormous detail, and by 1945 more than
six hundred studies had been completed: they covered
land reclamation (Pontine Marshes); overpopulation in
France; settlement possibilities in Baja California,
Negev, and Angola; Soviet nationalities policy in Central Asia; and colonization plans by Germans and Japanese in Eastern Europe and Java.[5]

Doomed by Roosevelt's death, Bowman's cautious-
ness, and Truman's lack of interest, the M-Project never
lived up to its billing and no International Settlement
Authority was ever created as its leaders had hoped. As
a result, the new United Nation Organization never became the grand central administrator of a rational colonization of the world that M-Project's sponsors had
dreamed about. Indeed, today almost no one knows of
its existence, and its interest lies in the realm of ideas
rather than achievements. A recent scholar has drawn

attention to the global geopolitical outlook that it embodied and that would become so central to American strategy in the Cold War. But my focus here is more specific. The M-Project is the backdrop against which we may evaluate the wartime shift in thinking on stabilizing European nationalism and preventing a future war—a shift that took policymakers away from international legal protection regimes and toward a territorialization of postwar planning. One of the consequences was the emergence of an independent Jewish national state in the Middle East as part of a "New Deal for the Middle East." This was an important development in its own right; but it was also the forerunner of the numerous other national states that the UN's General Assembly would recognize in the coming decades together with the refugee camps and displaced minorities that accompanied their emergence.[6]

⌐⊃

Amid the voluminous files of M-Project studies, there are references to the work of a little-remembered Russian Jewish demographer called Eugene Kulischer.[7] Kulischer produced studies of population displacement in Europe and of Jewish migration, and indeed he tended to see world history as the product of population movements. His English-language magnum opus, the 1948 *Europe on the Move, 1917–1947*, could be read as a distillation of the basic M-Project outlook and was in fact based on a number of wartime reports he had written for the International Labor Office, the Office of

Strategic Services, and the American Jewish Committee. Kulischer argued that population movements were "the mechanical foundations of history," and he saw a close connection over the centuries between war and migration, regarding the latter—caused by overpopulation—as a major source of international conflict. At its most basic, he suggested (giving Hegel a demographic twist), history was the story of the movement of races from east to west. In recent times, this westward drive of population had put pressure on Eastern Europe and Germany and threatened stability in Europe. The immigration quotas passed by the United States and other states between the wars had made matters worse and contributed to the breakdown of international order. Erecting barriers to migration was futile: they simply provoked conflict and would always do so. In the future, "millions in desperate search of outlets" could become "an aggressive force, especially if led by totalitarian governments."

The basic problem was that Europe was overpopulated—Kulischer argued—and the only solution was for its surplus to be settled in underdeveloped areas by regulated "migratory and colonizing movements." Progress in his terms was found when one obtained sustainable population growth, and this could be achieved best when Europe's surplus populations were exported so that "conflicts which might lead to war are reduced in volume or else channelled into colonial wars which take place at a safe distance from the metropolis." If war in Europe—in the circumstances of the early twentieth century—meant world war, exporting the continent's surplus population provided the only scientific guarantee of world peace. Kulischer shared with M-Project boss Isaiah Bowman a fundamental skepticism about whether organized global colonial settlement was really the answer: there was no longer enough land available for what he called "colonising conquest," and one could cite plenty of failed schemes that proved the futility of states trying to organize migration. In Kulischer's words, "The era of colonisation could not be revived." What was needed was the "rational redistribution of working power" regulated by an international planning authority.[8]

Kulischer's work was enormously wide-ranging in scope and did not focus on the Jews in particular; when he did write on Jewish refugee policy during the war, he emphasized the need to consider this within a more general framework of postwar reconstruction. Indeed his overarching theory of population movements (drawn from imperial Russian historian Vasili Kliuchevsky) tended not to differentiate between migration flows in general and forced population transfers in particular. The job of tracing the details of the latter, which were such a pronounced feature of wartime Nazi policy, Kulischer left to one of his M-Project colleagues, another Ukrainian Jew, called Joseph Schechtman.

Schechtman was also a recent arrival—having escaped from France only in 1941 before making his way to New York. He did not necessarily disagree with Kulischer's world-historical outlook, or his Eurocentrism, but his outlook was much more sharply focused on the plight of the Jews and his policy recommendations pushed in a very different direction. A few months after he arrived, Schechtman published a short pamphlet on the situation of Jews in German-held Soviet territory, and shortly after this he and Kulischer began undertaking research into migration with funding from the OSS, the International Labor Office, and the Institute for Jewish Affairs, a think-tank that had been set up to produce papers on issues relating to Jewish claims in an eventual postwar settlement. In 1944 and through much of 1945 Schechtman worked for the OSS as a specialist in issues of migration and forced population movements.[9]

Unlike Kulischer, Schechtman linked the demographic challenge of the 1940s to the specific political problem of nationalism. The nineteenth century was, as he put it, the "century of nationalities," and Europe still had to come to terms with how to create an international order compatible with this new philosophy. Between the wars it had tried minority rights. But Schechtman's chief wartime oeuvre—an immensely detailed study of forced population transfers that remains the standard work on the subject—was a blistering attack on the whole concept of minority protection. Unlike Kulischer and other wartime population experts, Schechtman believed that the League system had been proved entirely inadequate, and he openly doubted whether the problems of minorities were susceptible of "solution by legal means." Instead, peace would require "an ethnic shifting of the minorities. . . . These persons should be resettled where they can become a part of larger ethnic groups whose language they speak, to whose customs they have least antagonism, and to whom, spiritually, they owe allegiance." In the case of

Europe, that meant "transfer." It would not be necessary perhaps in all cases; sometimes, protection by an International Bill of Rights would suffice, or bilateral treaties— say between Hungary and Romania—would guarantee mutual good treatment. Nevertheless, "the drastic remedy of population transfer," as he put it, emerges as a desirable option, and the war's end provided in his judgment the perfect opportunity for decisive, radical measures.[10]

In fact, Schechtman had never much believed in the protection of international law, and an examination of his career reveals the close connections between social science scholarship and political activism that were characteristic of this epoch. Schechtman had been an activist from his school days, and not just any kind of activist either. He had been a vocal supporter of the right-wing Zionist Vladimir Jabotinsky since 1915, and after he left Kiev for the life of a political émigré in Berlin, Paris, and Warsaw, he was rarely far from his leader's side, writing editorials, helping run his Revisionist movement out of a tiny apartment, even delivering speeches to party organizations (including on one occasion in 1929 with Arthur Koestler). In short, he had lived a life at the very heart of Revisionist Zionism.[11]

Schechtman even had his own connection to Roosevelt's M-Project fantasies. Between 1937 and 1939, he had been Jabotinsky's "troubleshooter" in highly controversial negotiations with the Polish government to "evacuate" 1.5 million Jews from Poland; he also negotiated with the Polish government for an international conference to solve the question of Jewish settlement

outside Europe. Jabotinsky's New Zionist Organization
(NZO) expected such a conference to pressure the British into allowing a large-scale settlement in Palestine;
but the Poles, naturally, cared little where the Jews went
(all that mattered was that they should leave Europe)
and—like the British and indeed the Americans—were
keen to explore other options, from Madagascar to British Guiana. "A great Jewish Palestine does not lie in the
lines of traditional British policies," warned one proem-
igration Polish journalist. "However the establishment
of a Jewish territory in Africa may be in the political
and economic interests of the British Empire."[12]

Schechtman had tried to reassure other Zionists that
the result would not be a worldwide emigration and a
dispersal of forces, and he also rejected the charge that
the NZO wanted to liquidate Jewish life in Europe; the
bulk of Jews, he insisted in 1938, would always live
in the diaspora. But the Revisionists made two crucial
miscalculations—first, they thought the Poles had influence with the British over immigration to Palestine; and
second they believed the Poles did not mind the possibility of antagonizing the British. The entire Revisionist
scheme was thus premised on a refusal to take seriously
the threat of a German-initiated war that would bring
Poland and Britain together: indeed Jabotinsky himself
refused to believe this was imminent.[13]

In 1940 Jabotinsky arrived in New York—more than
a year before Schechtman—and he published a book a
few months later—the last before his sudden death—
that prefigured many of the themes implicit in Schechtman's analysis and introduced them to an American

Jewish audience. According to Jabotinsky, the League's minorities system was dead—across Eastern Europe—and could not be revived. The only hope for the Jews lay in being recognized as a separate nation by the Allies. Removing what he termed "the malignant ulcer" represented by "the Jewish tragedy" in East-Central Europe meant replacing naïve confidence in minority rights with an assertion of the Jews' rights to a national home of their own. "Racial peace in Poland—and not in Poland only—will be possible only as a corollary to a very extensive and greatly accelerated repatriation of Jewish masses to whatever spot on earth they may consider their national homeland." Demographic pressure made coexistence with Poles and others impossible; there were too many Jews for assimilation to succeed. Only with a mass "evacuation" would equal rights be imaginable for those who chose to stay behind. As for those worthy Roosevelt-inspired efforts at Evian and afterward to survey the globe for places where Jews could be settled, Jabotinsky was dismissive: Palestine offered the only practicable basis for a territorial solution and he cited Bowman's research to illustrate the point that alternative options did not exist. "Palestine, on both sides of the Jordan, is the only 'suitable' site for that Jewish state which, being the only remedy against Europe's cancer, is the world's urgent need." The Eurocentrism that had lain at the heart of Zionist thought since Herzl was never so urgently expressed as now, against the backdrop of the emergent Nazi New Order. Jabotinsky concluded by reviving his own version of an earlier settlement plan: there should be a massive and organized transfer of more than a million East European Jews to Palestine, under the aegis of the Intergovernmental Committee on Refugees, turning Jews into a majority there and securing the political future of the new Jewish state. As for the Arabs, unless they "choose to go away of their own accord, there is no need for them to emigrate." In Palestine, apparently, minority rights would be respected.[14]

Jabotinsky was still deeply mistrusted by mainstream Zionists, who accused him of fascist sympathies and disliked his toleration of the increasingly extreme nationalism of East European governments. But his evacuation scheme chimed in some ways with the kinds of ideas being pursued by the Roosevelt administration, and in 1939 he and Schechtman had discussed the subject with the American ambassadors in Warsaw and London.[15] Similar conversations were taking place elsewhere. The Polish ambassador in the United States, for example, held talks with Roosevelt that covered not merely Palestine but also the possibilities of large-scale settlement in Angola as a "supplemental Jewish homeland." And the Madagascar Plan, which the Nazis took up briefly in 1940, had also interested the Allies previously. We can thus see in these demographic blueprints the elements of an internationalist discourse circulating even across the frontlines in the ever-expanding world war. Indeed, when the chairman of the Jewish Agency's executive committee, David Ben Gurion, met Lord Moyne in London in 1941, the latter mentioned South America and Madagascar as possible destinations for those Jews willing and able to leave Europe. While the

Poles abandoned such schemes for the sake of their relationship with Britain, the territorialist option remained under serious investigation by American geographers envisaging a global New Deal not only for the Jews but for surplus European populations everywhere. In 1943 General Smuts joined in, calling for international management of Jewish refugee resettlement after the war, whether in Palestine or in former Italian colonies such as Libya and Eritrea. Consistent with Smuts's own desire to increase the number of Europeans settled in Africa, his proposal ran up against British objections on both political and economic grounds—by now Whitehall understood that settler colonialism in general was an expensive proposition for the modern state.[16]

But British objections would matter less than they once had because Jabotinsky's followers—Schechtman among them—were engineering the extraordinary transformation of American Jewish opinion that took place during the war and that put supporters of some kind of territorialist solution in a far stronger position politically than they had ever been before.[17] One indication of this was the erosion of belief in any revival of minority rights even among those who had supported the idea before the war. Jacob Robinson, for instance, was a Polish Jewish lawyer and demographer who had led the minorities bloc in the Lithuanian parliament in the 1920s; twenty years later, in exile in Manhattan, it was Robinson who founded the Institute of Jewish Affairs that employed both Kulischer and Schechtman. The latter's Revisionist background made him stand out at the institute; most of Robinson's closest colleagues were former Bundists or Russian liberals, sociologists and constitutional lawyers, men who had actively promoted interwar legal safeguards and believed that any postwar successor to the League should reaffirm the importance of international law. But by now they were on the defensive, and in 1943 they published a study plaintively entitled *Were the Minority Treaties a Failure?* This pleaded for greater understanding of what the architects of the League system had been trying to do; but revealingly it avoided pronouncing on the fundamental issue—of whether "minorities problems are by their nature capable of solution by legal means." This fact did not escape one of their reviewers, a tough-minded young University of Chicago political scientist named Hans Morgenthau. Summarizing the half-hearted arguments of *Were the Minority Treaties a Failure?* Morgenthau recounted the numerous obstacles the system had encountered and concluded—entirely in keeping with his Schmittian view of international politics—that what he dismissively called "legal instrumentalities" would "inevitably be used as tools by hostile nations in the contest for power." Less than a decade later, Morgenthau's antilegalist doctrine of "realism" would help shape the nascent discipline of international relations in the United States.[18]

⤚

At this point it may be helpful to spell out what this disdain for law meant for the future character of international organization. The late 1930s represented a moment of deep crisis for what remained of the Victorian concept of international—meaning European-based—civilization, especially for those professional jurists who had for the past half-century seen international law as the key instrument for promoting its values and moving toward a world that could rise above petty political differences. International legal norms had failed to win sufficient adherents to stem the move to war, or even to regulate the way it was waged, and the implications were frightening. Wolfgang Friedmann, a young émigré lawyer in London, was entirely representative of this mood in beholding in the rise of the Third Reich the "disintegration of European civilization itself" and in wondering what this presaged for the future role of law in a new international system. "Is European civilisation still what it was," he wondered, "and if not, how do the changes affect international law?"[19] "International law is seriously discredited and on the defensive," commented another. Cordell Hull, the U.S. secretary of state warned, in an address of June 1938, of a world growing internationally more and more "disordered and chaotic." One of his assistants, Francis Sayre, followed a few days later: "The supreme question which we and all the world face today is whether or not we are to live henceforth in a world of law or a world of international anarchy."

For men like Schechtman and Jabotinsky who had never reposed much confidence in international law, European civilization still defined the rules of the game but this game was driven by nationalism and only allowed for the effective protection of peoples when they were granted their own territory and state: without your own state, you were helpless. This was for the time a relatively extreme view and not one in either its external or its internal implications that the lawyers were likely to sympathize with. Most of them believed strongly that their discipline would still be needed after Nazism's defeat to prevent the emergence of the only alternative—"international anarchy." And they were inclined to see in the growth of unrestricted state power, of the rise of totalitarian and anti-individualistic ideologies of Left and Right, a powerful argument in favor of deploying the law more forcefully than ever to check the Hobbesian excesses of a sovereign power in its own territory.[20]

It was in this context that some of them veered round to advocating legal safeguards for *individual* human—as opposed to collective, minority—rights. But the wartime vogue for individualizing rights did not sweep the board, and older conceptions of the need to protect groups remained attractive. Indeed the man who, alongside Schechtman, wrote what may be the most enduring wartime study of the Nazi New Order, was an international lawyer who advocated a new and even tougher regime of legal safeguards that would extend to the actual criminalization of the persecution of minorities. This was Raphael Lemkin, another émigré, who arrived in the United States in 1941—the same year as Schechtman himself.

The German invasion of Poland had found Lemkin in Warsaw where he experienced what he later described as "a drop from civilisation to savagery." His family's house was burned and his mother was killed. German aircraft bombed the train on which he left Warsaw on 7 September, killing many of the passengers. Lemkin himself, despite a leg wound, continued his journey on foot; he had heard of plans to organize resistance behind the River Bug. Within days he was living in the forests, bearded and haggard, unable to sleep and losing blood. But eventually he made his way to the relative safety of Sweden where he lectured at the University of Stockholm and began to compile the enormous collection of decrees issued by the Nazi occupation authorities across Europe that formed the basis for his subsequent research. Sweden had remained neutral during the war, and Lemkin with his customary tenacity, persuaded Swedish consuls in occupied Europe to send him back copies of published German orders and commands.[21]

Several years earlier, he had met and befriended an American law professor from Duke University, Michael McDermott, who was teaching in Warsaw. McDermott was now instrumental in arranging an invitation for Lemkin to come to the States. Catching an eastbound train from Moscow he made his way via Japan and arrived in North Carolina in April 1941. Once America entered the war, his encyclopedic knowledge of German administrative law became invaluable to Washington and he moved there, lecturing in military government to the U.S. Army and acting as consultant to Henry Wallace's Bureau of Economic Warfare. The Carnegie Endowment subsidized the publication of his book, *Axis Rule in Occupied Europe*, in 1944. Together with Schechtman's study of forced population movements, it remains one of the indispensable works on the Nazi New Order published at the time.

The spirit animating *Axis Rule in Occupied Europe*, however, was very different from Schechtman's. Lemkin denounced Nazi violence as the product of a set of techniques of government as administered by a modern nationalizing state. Analyzing the Germans through their own wartime laws and decrees, Lemkin conveyed the purposeful and bureaucratic character of this manner of waging war. *Genocide* was the term coined by Lemkin in this book for the destruction of national or ethnic groups. It would subsequently enter common parlance and international law because it offered a way for understanding mass violence as part of deliberate state policy. Lemkin insisted that "genocide" needed to be seen as a whole; it was a "composite" of different acts of persecution and destruction. Some of these had been classed as violations of the laws of war in the Hague Regulations of 1907. But the Germans had introduced others as well, which collectively made the nineteenth-century assumption that war was waged against sovereigns and armies, and not against civilians, outdated. He noted, for example, how in Poland, they kept the price of alcohol low and encouraged abortions as part of the goal of diminishing the Slavic population. "The entire problem of genocide," he concluded, "is too important to be left for piecemeal discussion and solution in the future." After all, as he pointed out, this was not merely a problem of war but also of peace—especially in Europe, with its hodgepodge of different ethnic groups and perennial border disputes.

Only a reassertion and reinvigoration of international law could, in Lemkin's view, prevent such crimes from recurring. The task of the United Nations—as he put it— was to create such political and spiritual conditions after the war "that the Germans will be impelled to replace their theory of master race by a theory of master morality, international law and true peace." This was international law in the service of that Tolstoyan ideal of moral renovation that had animated him since boyhood.

Unfortunately such an approach now ran counter to the prevailing mood in official circles. Swimming against the tide, Lemkin himself experienced these reservations firsthand in the immediate postwar years, when he acted as adviser to the chief U.S. prosecutor at Nuremberg and later as adviser on foreign affairs to the Department of War (1945–47). The UN War Crimes Commission had had a troubled history; indeed its vicissitudes provided an early indication that the great powers sponsoring the new peacetime United Nations Organization had strong doubts about making international criminal law a prominent part of the new world order. As late as October 1944, it seemed likely that restrictive definitions of German culpability would preclude Nazi defendants being tried for crimes against German citizens. Henry Stimson, the U.S. secretary of war and the main advocate of a legal approach to the punishment of German war crimes was far more interested in criminalizing aggressive war—something he had sought since the interwar years. As it was, intense discussions among the powers in the summer of 1945 did establish that "crimes against humanity" would form part of the charter of the

International Military Tribunal, but Lemkin himself was disappointed that although they were included in the indictment, the eventual judgment failed to mention them outside the context of "aggressive war" and did not appear to regard Germany's persecution of its Jewish population before the war as within its purview.[22]

Even before the tribunal delivered its verdict, Lemkin advocated turning the legal regime of the new United Nations into a tougher version of the League's minorities system. In May 1946 he contacted the newly appointed secretary-general Trygve Lie to highlight the need to "intervene in internal affairs of other countries on behalf of persecuted minorities." A few months later, he was lobbying delegates in Paris meeting to draw up the peace treaties with the former Axis satellites and submitting proposals that they include provisions allowing minorities to appeal to the United Nations and allowing the UN to impose sanctions where it deemed necessary. In Paris, his lobbying fell on deaf ears: it was hard enough for the British, French, Americans, and Russians to agree even without introducing a deeply unpopular proposal—one that conjured up memories of past failures. But he was more successful in the run-up to the first General Assembly meeting at the end of 1946, and thanks to the support of the Indian and South American delegates, he managed to get a genocide resolution placed on the agenda for New York. On 11 December 1946, the assembly called for a convention on genocide to be prepared and from thenceforth until his death, Lemkin acted in effect as a one-man lobbyist for the Genocide Convention. His crusade encountered opposition, of course, yet Lemkin himself was a formidable advocate. Not only did he manage to get a draft convention through the Economic and Social Council but he also organized a major lobbying campaign by NGOs as the Third General Assembly met to consider the Convention in Paris in 1948. That December—one day before the Declaration of Human Rights was voted through—the convention was adopted unanimously, but that only committed Lemkin to further rounds of lobbying in order to get the convention ratified, something he managed to do within two years.[23]

Much of the recent literature on the history of human rights hails Lemkin's achievement in pushing through the convention and frames it as part of the UN's broader inaugural commitment to human rights. Yet this approach may lose sight of what was distinctive and even quixotic about this story. As Lemkin himself noted at the time, his crusade (a word he himself often used) was opposed not only by the usual suspects among official delegations, and not only by those alienated by his prickly, vainglorious, and suspicious temperament, but more pertinently, by other international lawyers who differed sharply with him about how best to protect rights under the United Nations. Lemkin was still thinking in the same way he had done before the war—that is to say, of providing international legal protection for minorities, with international law this time being given criminal sanctions. Others felt such an approach might arouse all the political reservations (notably, over the infringement of the principle of state sovereignty) that had been associated with the minority rights treaties, and thus strain the international support that existed for the UN more generally. The relationship between the Genocide Convention and the Universal Declaration of Human Rights that the General Assembly passed at the same time, reflects this divergence; far from representing part of a single scheme as some historians have suggested, the two measures stood for very different approaches to the role of law in international life. One was an elaboration of the interwar regime; the other gestured toward a much weaker regime, whose ardent rhetoric of moral aspiration was supposed in some measure to act as substitute for the force of law. And as it was, the Genocide Convention itself only passed once a clause that made "cultural genocide" a crime—the clause that Lemkin himself described as the "soul of the Convention"—was dropped. Resolute opposition from colonial powers and South American states in particular thus prevented minority rights being smuggled into the UN by the back door.[24]

It was in fact unusual for the United Nations to involve itself directly in the formulation of international law, for the new body was warier of pronouncing on the subject than its predecessor had been. Many of the lawyers who had tried to pressure the League into setting up an international criminal court in the 1930s did the same with the UN; but the Security Council displayed little interest in the idea.[25] And despite the whittling down of the Genocide Convention's scope from the original draft prepared in the UN Secretariat's legal section, it still represented the kind of potentially far-reaching intervention in the domestic jurisdiction of member states that so many of the UN's founders had feared.

The decision of the General Assembly to push for a convention on genocide at all showed that interventionism was certainly not defunct in the new world organization. Yet it was a rare and incomplete foray in this direction, and one whose value many of Lemkin's fellow lawyers remained uncertain about. Even some of those who worked with him on the first draft of the convention in 1947 believed that the age of protecting minorities through law had passed; it was better perhaps to take advantage of the world's new interest in individual *human* rights and to rely on shaping public opinion. *This* was the rationale behind the Universal Declaration of Human Rights. As has been shown in a fascinating recent piece of research, 1948 thus saw an outright clash between Lemkin, on the one hand, and the drafters of the Universal Declaration on the other. Partly, this arose over their anxieties that the United States—where the Senate was already jittery about foreign meddling in domestic affairs, especially in the South—would certainly not ratify a future covenant on human rights if confronted with something as binding as the Genocide Convention.

Lemkin—in his opponents' eyes—had not realized that the world had changed, that international law could no longer claim a position above politics, and that it had lost much of its strength—in short, that where international law was concerned, the world of the UN was very different from that of the League. One scholar plausibly suggests that the reason why so many people at the UN became irritated with Lemkin was not merely his persistence (eventually not far short of paranoia) and intensity of focus but that he stood for a past which they were trying to avoid mentioning. And indeed it cannot escape our notice that precisely as the Genocide Convention was wending its way through the various organs of the UN in the late 1940s, the prewar minority rights treaties were quietly and unobtrusively laid to rest.[26]

The passing of the convention seemed like Lemkin's moment of triumph. But the voting down of the cultural genocide clause revealed the deep misgivings many states had at allowing their own actions to be brought before an international court. Once passed, the convention fell into abeyance, and became little more than a plaything of the Cold War confrontation. No international penal tribunal was set up as it had envisaged and its existence on paper did nothing to deter the numerous examples of state-organized violence that erupted in the 1950s and 1960s across the world. The United States refused to ratify it and as Lemkin tried increasingly desperately to get it to do so, he played more and more shamelessly to the anticommunist gallery. (In fact, American ratification did not come until 1986, and then only with substantial reservations.) Thus although the convention itself entered into effect in 1951, it would be hard to argue that it did much to deter mass violations of collective rights. The same fundamental reluctance to give the UN human rights regime real enforceability was evident in the fate of the 1948 Declaration of Human Rights as well. In this case, the step towards a convention or an international bill was never taken at all, and it was left—as calmer minds than Lemkin's had predicted—to regional organizations, notably the Council of Europe, to make a human rights regime legally enforceable.

⌒

If this was to be the dismal fate of the League's legalistic approach to collective rights in the new world order of the UN, what then of the robustly territorialist vision represented by Revisionist Zionism? Here is where it is necessary to return to Schechtman. Like Lemkin, this wartime analyst also found himself in the role of post-war advocate, but for a very different cause. In 1946 he published his classic work on the Nazis' demographic policies—*European Population Transfers, 1939–1945*, which, as mentioned earlier, constituted an argument for transfer as well as an analysis of it. Events were making Schechtman's point for him, for the demography of Eastern Europe was being altered under the Allies even more sweepingly than it had been under the Nazis—more than 12 million Germans were uprooted, as well as millions of Ukrainians, not to mention Poles, Hungarians, Slovaks, Albanians, and others, in a series of expulsions and exchanges that were tolerated if not instigated by the Big Three.

In Zionist circles, transfer was the policy that still dared not speak its name, an obvious solution to an unwanted problem that could not be publicly acknowledged without harming the cause. The hidden and intermittent history of this idea has been traced to before the outbreak of the Second World War.[27] Future president of Israel Chaim Weizmann had pondered a "quasi-exchange of populations," and the Jewish Agency set up a secret Population Transfer Committee in 1937, at a time when British partition proposals encouraged thoughts in this direction. The official British Peel Commission report of the same year had recommended a population exchange, recalling the compulsory 1923 exchange between Greece and Turkey that had involved some 2 million people, and urging further investigation into whether there was sufficient land to resettle Arabs—whether voluntarily or not—from what would become the "Jewish State." Ben Gurion himself told the Jewish Agency Executive that he supported the idea. Yet many Zionists were dubious and the American Jewish leader Stephen Wise denounced the idea of a forced population exchange as "a menace to Jewish life in the Galuth [Diaspora]. . . . a boomerang we are hurling into the heart of our people," precisely because it would lead to "an ending of the safeguarding of minorities everywhere." On the eve of the war, therefore, diaspora Jewish support for a regime of minorities' protection was still strong, and concern for the plight of Jews in Europe and elsewhere outweighed the hopes for national consolidation in Palestine. A reversal of British policy pointed in the same direction: the White Paper of May 1939 effectively turned the Peel Commission's recommendations on their head, promising the Arab majority in mandatory Palestine independence within a decade, and by implication envisaging the Jews as a protected minority. Even advocates of transfer preferred not to voice the idea openly, well aware that with the emergence of nation-states across the former Ottoman provinces of the Arab lands, Palestinian Arabs were starting to acquire a national consciousness of their own.[28]

Yet Nazi wartime policies changed everything, as Weizmann and Ben Gurion both instantly realized. Speaking in January 1941 to the Russian ambassador in London, the former raised the subject of transferring a million Arabs to Iraq and replacing them with 4 to 5 million Jews from Poland and Russia. In April 1941, he noted that "after this war the whole problem of exchanges of populations will not be such a taboo subject as it has before. It is going on now, and probably will become part and parcel of the future settlement. I don't say that the Arabs of Palestine will have to go to Iraq or Transjordan, but the fact remains that for every one Arab that goes out, four Jews can step in. . . . It is not a problem which one would shirk at the end of this war. This change in old values will take place and I believe we don't have to be too timid about it." In public, to be sure, he was still guarded. In an article in *Foreign Affairs*, he talked about the Middle East's need for "guidance" and "development" and touched lightly on the idea of a voluntary transfer for any Arabs not wishing to stay in the Jewish state. But in private, he was much less restrained. As for Ben Gurion, he made it plain that while transfer must not appear to be "a Jewish proposal," it was not something he opposed.[29]

In the United States, the long-time leader of the American Zionist movement, Stephen Wise, had always been dubious. As for non-Zionist grandees like Felix

Warburg, they placed their money on conciliating the Arabs with large-scale development proposals that would encourage but not compel emigration across the Jordan. It was the Biltmore conference in 1942, with its call for the postwar establishment of a Jewish national home, that marked American Zionism's march toward a more hard-nosed attitude increasingly suspicious of all schemes premised on Arab-Jewish cooperation. At Biltmore, American Jewry swung behind the idea that "the new world order" required solving the problem of "Jewish homelessness" and talked about turning Palestine into a "Jewish Commonwealth." Wise was replaced by Abba Hillel Silver—a man much more sympathetic to the vigor of Revisionism—and the first articles began to appear in the Jewish press calling for a population transfer between Palestine and Iraq.[30]

The Revisionists, one should note, were not leading the charge for transfer. On the contrary, Jabotinsky and Schechtman had always insisted that their evacuation plan for Polish Jewry would be voluntary and leave large numbers in the diaspora. One of the virtues of their demand for an unrestricted immigration policy into a large Israel occupying both sides of the Jordan, Jabotinsky insisted, was that a large Jewish majority there would have nothing to fear from the Arab minority inside its borders; compulsory evacuation would simply be unnecessary. Schechtman admits that they sympathized with the idea of a "voluntary and organised migration" of the Arab population to a neighboring country—but after all, which Zionist did not? Yet the war changed the Revisionist outlook too: in November

1939, shortly after hearing about the first Nazi transfers of ethnic Germans—from the Baltic states "back" to the Reich—the previous month, Jabotinsky wrote to a colleague that "there is no choice: the Arabs must make room for the Jews in Eretz Israel. If it is possible to transfer the Baltic peoples, it is also possible to move the Palestinian Arabs." The Nazis were demonstrating the undreamed-of possibilities of demographic engineering for nationalist ends—Schechtman in his book would count more than fifty separate wartime forced evacuations in occupied Europe—and simultaneously demonstrating in a way not even Jabotinsky had imagined the existential threat to East European Jewry in particular.[31]

By the time the war was over, Weizmann's prophecy had been borne out. The world had become used to the idea of population transfer and fewer objections were raised to the use of "Hitlerite methods" than earlier. Mainstream American public opinion now freely discussed the idea of a New Deal for world peace that would necessarily encompass population transfers to eradicate sources of ethnic tension and, simultaneously, even out population densities and spur growth. In private, Roosevelt had talked about putting up "barbed wire around Palestine" and moving the Arabs to "some other part of the Middle East," somewhere with sufficient water supplies to support them. Former president Herbert Hoover was less restrained: he publicly called for an organized population transfer, to the delight of the American Zionist leadership, while experts extolled the possibilities of the "great alluvial plains of the Tigris and Euphrates valley." Henry Wallace, in his role as editor of the *New Republic* in 1946, was only one of many calling for a "sound economic program for the whole Near East" on such lines. Thus the New Deal for the World outlined in a recent book by Elizabeth Borgwardt actually incorporated both progressivism and coercion, a vision of state-led rationalization that existed alongside and sometimes trumped individual human rights.[32]

Schechtman himself now briefly resumed activity within the leadership of the Revisionist movement (which rejoined the world Zionist movement in 1946) and became head of its chief policymaking committee even as his pathbreaking work on wartime *European Population Transfers* came out to positive reviews. The flight of large numbers of Palestinian Arabs in the following months, which accelerated once war broke out in May 1948, made his specialism more timely than ever and led the Israeli ambassador to the United States to encourage him to provide propaganda materials on the Arab refugees.[33]

The question was especially urgent because both the UN mediator, Count Bernadotte, and President Truman were putting pressure on the new Israeli government to permit the return of Palestinian refugees. The Israeli foreign minister, Moshe Shertok, knew of Schechtman—the Jewish Agency had recently funded a research trip of his to Poland—and sought to accelerate the publication of his new study of postwar transfers. Schechtman now visited Israel and met members of the official Transfer Committee, who also asked for his help. One of its members, Jewish National Fund Lands Division head

Yosef Weitz, had been pushing for transfer since the 1930s. As Arab villagers were evicted from their homes for reasons of wartime security, and then discouraged or prevented from returning, Weitz was already thinking about formulating an organized "transfer policy" and won foreign minister Shertok's approval. On 4 June, his committee convened to discuss what he described as "the miracle" of the Arab exodus "and how to make it permanent." Although Ben Gurion dithered about backing a full transfer policy, Weitz remained keen and by August the Foreign Ministry was resolved to prevent the return of Arab refugees. On 29 August, Weitz's appointment as member of the Transfer Committee was approved by the cabinet, and in December, the month after Schechtman's visit, the committee recommended settling the refugees in "thinly-populated" Iraq, Syria, and Transjordan. Not the least of the advantages of this policy was that it might speed up the flow of Jews from Arab lands, something that the Zionist leadership was increasingly anxious to ensure as it became clear that many European survivors would not willingly come to Palestine. The following year, Schechtman authored two booklets advocating the committee's resettlement plans, which the Jewish Agency published and which remained stock propaganda items for some time.[34]

In 1949, a few months after his return from Israel, Schechtman's *Population Transfers in Asia* was published, discreetly subsidized by the Jewish Agency. If his magnum opus of three years earlier had confined its verdict on the merits of transfer to its concluding pages, this work did not. Not surprisingly in view of its sponsors, as Schechtman moved from Europe to Asia, so he became more prescriptive. Having covered what he described as the "Hindu-Moslem exchange of populations" in India, and the fate of Armenians and Assyrian Christians, fully half of the book was devoted to his "Case for Arab-Jewish Transfer of Population." "Palestine," Schechtman wrote, "seems a classic case for quick, decisive transfer action as the only constructive method of solving the basic problem and preventing extremely dangerous developments." Partition itself was a half measure that "merely limits, but by no means solves, the crucial and explosive problem of Palestine's minorities." There was nothing unusual in "the idea of Arabs moving from one area to another," and plenty of precedents were to be found in Europe's own history, especially in Turkey's "repatriation" of Muslims from the Balkans. What was more, Iraq in particular was—according to Schechtman—suffering from low population growth and desperately in need of the injection of resources represented by Palestinian Arabs. The book concluded by affirming that an "exchange of minorities" was "not only the most promising but actually the only possible solution of the Arab-Jewish deadlock." Schechtman outlined what this would look like: "As a rule, every Arab in the Jewish state, and every Jew in Iraq or any other Arab country would be subject to transfer"; only those who asked explicitly to be exempted from the agreement would be allowed to stay, provided they pledged full allegiance to the country they remained in. Even then, they would lose all minority rights, and the government concerned would have the right to deport them on security grounds. To all intents and purposes, this was an obligatory population exchange along the lines of that brokered under the League of Nations between Greece and Turkey in 1923. The idea of minority rights had vanished as though it had never existed.

The times had seemingly validated the views of Schechtman and the Revisionists. The UN Charter made no mention of minorities, and the subject had been ignored at San Francisco; as the conference met, Germans were being expelled from Czechoslovakia and the eastern provinces of the Reich. The Potsdam conference the same summer had ratified this expulsion, and Hungarian efforts to bring back minorities protection the following year failed. The UN went so far as to create a subcommission on the prevention of discrimination and protection of minorities in 1947 but it was quickly marginalized.[35] Schechtman himself was keenly aware of what he called the new "political climate" of the United Nations. Charting its waning interest in protecting minorities, he noted approvingly in 1951 that its sponsoring powers were extremely reluctant to repeat what they regarded as the errors of the League on this question. The League's protection regime had been scrapped, and the UN instead focused—weakly—on the prevention of discrimination rather than on legally mandated safeguards. For all the rhetoric about human rights, the mood in the General Assembly was for enforced assimilation and against any mechanisms that might retard this since new and old states alike agreed that minorities had undermined the stability of Europe. Schechtman noted that the UN was tackling minorities questions in an "essentially dilatory way." The 1948 Declaration of Human Rights had not mentioned minorities at all. (And, as we have seen, the Genocide Convention had been stripped of the clause on cultural genocide that threatened to reintroduce minority rights under another name). When the UN created successor regimes in former Italian colonies, it resisted calls to make specific provisions protecting minorities. The one exception, ironically, had been the 1947 General Assembly resolution that called for the partition of Palestine. This had explicitly provided for cultural and educational rights for the minorities in the two states, as well as for the continued usage—along Ottoman lines—of family and inheritance law customary to the community. Yet here too there was no proposal to monitor compliance by the states concerned—a U.S. proposal suggesting a UN *guarantee* got nowhere—and in any event, the resolution was quickly overtaken by events.[36]

⥲

What should we conclude from this story of wartime Jewish scholarship and advocacy? In the first place, we should remember the extent to which the UN discussions came out of earlier arguments rehearsed at the League. All of those involved—and certainly both Schechtman and Lemkin—were deeply influenced by the events of First World War and its aftermath. The League of Nations had combined a Victorian faith in the power of international law and diplomatic treaties with a new Wilsonian commitment to national self-determination; for the Jews in particular, it had offered both minority rights and Balfour's pledge of a national home in Palestine. The two men both wanted to rescue what was valuable in the League's approach, but differed over what that was.

It was Schechtman who won out. By the end of the Second World War, mainstream European opinion had come round to the view that he had espoused for years. Faith in international law was badly dented, and across the board the UN retreated from the interventionist approach that had characterized the League. The retreat from minority rights formed part of this phenomenon—the scrapping of the minorities treaties and the evisceration of the Genocide Convention. Minorities were now seen as sources of destabilization, and liberals and socialists were as passionate in demanding their eradication as fascists. At Liberation, expulsions—not only of Germans, but also of Ukrainians, Poles, and others in Eastern Europe—were widely seen as the lesser evil and were condoned by the Allies and Stalin. In effect, everyone had come around to the nationalist cause: what the Revisionists and the Nazis had called for in the 1930s, the Allies now promoted—ethnic homogeneity as a desirable feature of national self-determination and international stability.

All of those whose views I have discussed here agreed on something else too. Europe's problems were the world's problems, and the rest of the world was there to ensure that Europe was stabilized. For M-Project planners, that meant a scheme of international settlement—in effect, globalizing the Smutsian vision, using Europe's surplus population as refugees. For Zionists, it meant creating a Jewish nation-state in Palestine. Israel was, as it were, the realization of M-Project logic. If I have not cited a single Arab voice here, it is because their voices—which were certainly being raised in protest—were almost entirely ignored in these discussions. Arab populations were regarded as malleable in a way that the Jews were not, and if Palestinian Arabs did not welcome the prospect of becoming a minority in a Jewish nation-state, then surely they could move elsewhere in the Middle East. After all, so the reasoning went, a state of Jewish settlers would, if guided in the right way, act as a civilizing force for the region as a whole, spearheading a new model of growth and development. That Eurocentrism was alive and well was thus underscored by the very formation of Israel.

In this process the United Nations played a major role. Palestine only came before the UN once the 1945 Labor government took the basic decision to wash its hands of its fate. Once there, it became a rare example of an issue over whose future Washington and Moscow could find agreement, partly because neither yet saw the Middle East as nearly as important as Europe. Despite violent internal disagreements among its members, the United Nations in 1947 backed the proposal for partition and two years later it went further and granted UN membership to the new state of Israel.

In so doing, it functioned very differently from its predecessor. After the First World War, the shapers of international order had been hesitant about allowing the proliferation of unsupervised small states; now the United Nations threw its weight behind their emergence and turned itself into the guarantor of their legitimacy. Supporting the UN partition plan at the assembly discussions in October 1947, the Soviet delegate had argued that "in the circumstances, juridical and historical arguments should play only a secondary part . . . the essence of the question was the right of self-determination." It was not surprising that Ben Gurion's Israel—in its 1948 declaration of independence—appealed explicitly to the United Nations in affirming its right to exist. American recognition was one vital step to international acceptance; but membership of the United Nations was a crucial mark of legitimacy as well.[37]

It was just the start. Decolonization brought more and more nationalist claims to self-determination, and the confederal innovations by which the British and French tried in the 1940s to hold their colonies together soon disintegrated. The dream of a single confederal Palestine was thus not the only such vision to fail. Even anticolonial movements that appealed to broader allegiances such as Pan-Africanism and Pan-Arabism were torn apart by national interests, their newly independent members fiercely contesting efforts at creating powerful regional or even continentwide polities.[38] Such states proliferated in the Middle East, South Asia, and sub-Saharan Africa, and as a result, the membership of the UN grew by leaps and bounds—at a rate unimagined by its wartime founders—from 51 in 1945 to 117 two decades later and 189 by the century's end. This expansion was seen by anticolonial activists in positive terms, and in 1960 found its expression in the UN General Assembly's Declaration on Granting Independence to Colonial Countries and Peoples. The declaration talked about freedom and human rights and warned that the perpetuation of colonial rule threatened world peace. But it said nothing about minorities. It talked without qualification about the right of *all* peoples to self-determination, but denounced the "partial or total disruption of the national unity and territorial integrity of a country." As wars in Biafra, Morocco, Eritrea, and Bangladesh demonstrated, rather a lot of questions were begged by this extravagantly Wilsonian language. The emergence of these Third World states thus expanded and intensified the sway of nationalism, often accompanied by the same phenomena that had been seen in Eastern Europe—partition, population flight, and the creation of refugees. In short, postwar decolonization represented a globalization of the problem—nationalism—that Roosevelt's M-Project planners had been considering in 1941. Their solution—a global New Deal based on Western money and know-how—never materialized.

This story may help us understand the decisiveness of the postwar shift away from minority rights. Initially this had reflected changing great power preferences. The League had only monitored the behavior of "new states," because Britain, the United States, and France saw minority rights as an element in shoring up the cordon sanitaire they had created in Eastern Europe. After 1945, they had neither the capacity nor the desire to do this any longer in the region, still less anywhere else;

and of course they remained as insistent as they had been in 1919 that their own internal affairs were not to be subject to discussion. Indeed the fear that African American civil rights leaders might use minority rights machinery at the UN to embarrass the United States simply confirmed Washington's dislike of any activist rights regime. In 1947, for instance, the National Association for the Advancement of Colored People presented the UN with its petition denouncing the treatment of blacks in the United States; the new UN Commission on Human Rights chose not to investigate. At the same time, the UN's new member states supported the tendency to protect sovereignty from international intervention, and as a result, the UN never developed the interest or expertise in monitoring the plight of minorities that its predecessor had done.[39]

Schechtman dreamed of eradicating the problem of minorities completely through all-encompassing compulsory population exchanges in the Middle East and South Asia. So far as he was concerned, the partitions of the late 1940s had left both situations unresolved: there were still Arabs in Israel and Jews in Arab states, Muslims in India and Hindus in Pakistan. Although all-encompassing agreements were hard to reach—often because the states concerned did not have good enough relations—Schechtman's dislike of minorities and his desire to make them disappear fit the mood of the postwar years better than the alternative. To many in the 1950s, Lemkin's advocacy of the criminalization of genocide seemed at the time a return to the past way of doing things, not a new way forward. There was something nineteenth-century about his vision of a world in which cultural diversity would be protected through the authority of international law, expressing the will of a global community determined to check the crimes of national politicians. Lemkin himself believed wholeheartedly in the primacy of European civilization. But the regime of international law that had reflected such attitudes was on the wane, and efforts to draw up an International Bill of Human Rights through the UN resulted only in a declaration that was—in the words of one of the most eminent legal commentators of the day—"without legal force and of controversial moral authority."[40] Even the Genocide Convention did little to protect minorities after 1945 from assault and massive violence. Were one unkind, one might say that it was merely the homage paid by the United Nations to the impotence of its predecessor and to the victims of the Nazis. The awkward truth was that the UN had abandoned the League's commitment, however faltering, to protecting minorities, without willing an effective alternative. It would take Cambodia, Bosnia, and Rwanda to drive the point home.

4
Chapter §

Jawaharlal Nehru and the Emergence of the Global United Nations

The founders of the new United Nations deliberately played down any hint of continuity between the new world organization and the League. Reviewing the quiet winding up of the League in April 1946, one American commentator (and drafter of the Charter) noted the "hesitancy in many quarters to call attention to the essential continuity of the old League and the new United Nations for fear of arousing latent hostilities or creating doubts which might seriously jeopardize the birth and early success of the new organization." But the continuities were striking: the truth is that the UN was, despite its very different attitude to minority rights, "essentially a second League of Nations."[1]

Like the League, the UN was basically a cooperative grouping of independent states. Explicit where the League was implicit, it rested on the doctrine of the sovereign equality of its members. Yet despite the utopian rhetoric of its supporters, the UN represented a deliberate retreat from the League's comparative egalitarianism back to the great power conclaves of the past. The General Assembly had, in general, *less* power than the League's assembly had done and the five permanent members of the Security Council had more. They were equipped with their new veto-wielding prerogative, and to facilitate the policing role that Roosevelt had emphasized, they also gave themselves the power to call on their own military staff to coordinate security measures for the sake of world peace. In other words, the UN, even more than the League, was to be run by the great powers and far less confidence was reposed in international law as a set of norms independent from, and standing above, power politics. On the contrary, as a Soviet lawyer wrote, international law now implicitly recognized "special rights" (and special obligations) for the "great peace-loving states."[2]

As for the UN's attitude to colonialism, this appeared at the outset to be little less tolerant than the League's had been. Mandates were renamed trusteeships, and the Charter gave the General Assembly somewhat more extensive supervisory powers over most of the latter than had existed in the earlier version: the petitions process was more serious than it had been, the assembly was granted oversight of trusteeship administration, and the Trusteeship Council could arrange on-site visits. But only 20 million people inhabited trusteeships compared with several hundred millions in European colonies, now euphemistically known as Non-Self-Governing Territories, and half-hearted American proposals to put *all* colonies under UN control were rejected. Indeed European powers were reasserting their control over their colonial possessions in Southeast Asia even as the San Francisco conference met, and American anticolonial rhetoric dwindled as the war came to a close and the importance of good transatlantic relations with the major West European powers became obvious in Washington.

Whatever the rhetoric, therefore, this was an international organization designed—much as its predecessor had been—for interstate cooperation and stability in a world of empires and great powers. The British delegate unashamedly told the conference that it was the existence of their colonial empires that had saved the European powers from defeat; they had become "one vast machine for the defence of liberty," and it was surely inconceivable to imagine breaking this up.[3]

One notable difference for those familiar with the working of the old League was the much diminished role of the European states themselves. The war had left the continent devastated and the impact on its standing in international affairs was immediately felt even before delegates moved from the warmth of California to the drab streets of London and Paris. "In the League of Nations," wrote one League supporter from San Francisco, "the European countries played a predominant part . . . in San Francisco many European countries were not represented at all. . . . The emergence of an American bloc . . . coincides oddly with the end of the legendary belief in the bloc of the British Commonwealth." Georges Bidault, the French foreign minister, was struck by the same thing a few months later. "It is a remarkable fact . . . to note the extent to which Europe is absent," he noted as he surveyed the faces at the first General Assembly meeting in London. Churchill's wartime desire for a world organization to run Europe—a kind of new Concert of Three—had been rejected by both Roosevelt and Stalin. The result was an organization that in spirit if not in form represented a very different world from the League.[4]

Was this the reason for the powerful current of anti-colonial sentiment that rose to the surface in 1946 in the General Assembly? Perhaps: the Americans in particular—both south and north—were staunchly anticolonial; so were the USSR and its allies, China, the Philippines, and many of the Arab states. Yet it was not this factor so much as internal frictions among Commonwealth members that were responsible for pushing the UN decisively in a direction largely unforeseen by its sponsors. As frictions multiplied—over Palestine, India, Burma—London, the center of Smuts's Commonwealth, no longer held sway. Palestine was deliberately handed over by the British to the UN to sort out. India was not, but it made its presence felt there anyway, as we will see. As the UN was drawn in to adjudicate on intraimperial dissensions it was itself transformed. Having started out thanks to its great power architects as an institution tolerant of empire—it would take, said Roosevelt's undersecretary of state Sumner Welles—"a thousand years for Portuguese Timor to gain independence"— it turned astonishingly quickly into a key forum for anticolonialism.[5]

Once again Smuts—now nearing the end of his political life—and South Africa found themselves at the center of events. In fact, it would be little exaggeration to say that it was over South Africa and its policies that the global possibilities inherent in the United Nations institutions first emerged. First, there was a debate over the future of South-West Africa—the League mandate that Smuts still hoped to annex. Second there was the issue of Indians in South Africa itself and the growing official discrimination to which they were subjected. In 1946, even before India itself gained independence, Jawaharlal Nehru and his interim government seized on this and turned it into a cause célèbre, bypassing Whitehall and publicizing their case in the UN General Assembly. This chapter charts the result—the beginning of the transformation of the UN into the global forum that it remains today. While South Africa turned toward apartheid and became an international pariah by clinging to race politics, India emerged as the first successful challenger of the doctrine of the European right to rule and highlighted the emerging influence (but also the limits to that influence) of a new element in the international system—the postcolonial world.

In 1945 Jan Smuts still hoped to fulfill South Africa's geopolitical destiny by expanding northward and creating a Greater South Africa. Far from regarding this as an anachronism, he understood the Second World War as the struggle that would enable this expansion to take place. Better from his perspective a continent under South African guidance within the British Commonwealth than either of the alternatives—a Nazi-dominated *Euroafrika* of the kind being pedaled in the war years by German colonial enthusiasts, or the anarchy and fragmentation he anticipated with any serious concession to native rule. Smuts expected that his prompt response to the German attack on Poland—winning the crucial vote in Parliament and bringing South Africa into the war alongside Britain—would win him support in London for his goals. But in Whitehall, sentiment had changed since the early years of the century, and the

British were fully cognizant of black African opposition to any extension of white South African political control, either during the war or after it. They rebuffed Smuts in October 1939 and continued to do so thereafter.

Yet Smuts did not see any insuperable obstacle—perhaps because influential policymakers in London and Washington sympathized with his arguments. At home it was a different story: there his wartime federalist vision for sub-Saharan Africa—fully in keeping with the broader wartime vogue for federalist solutions for the postwar world as a whole—split his white followers. The English-language press largely approved, and the *Natal Daily News* gave a modernizer's justification for South Africa to take the lead. This was not, it insisted, a return to the bad old days. On the contrary, "The old era of imperialism [is] giving way to a period when capital and technical services would be made available for the development of less advanced territories." Other journalists recognized that South Africa's appalling reputation for its native policy needed to be changed before there could be any hope of an "African confederation." But Afrikaner opinion was not easily persuaded. For many Afrikaners, Smuts's grandiose dreams of continental leadership were frightening and his policy would lead to them "being swallowed up by a great Black State controlled by foreign [in other words British] elements." This was Smuts's tightrope: to carry London with him while not losing Afrikaner backing at home. What black Africans thought scarcely entered into the equation.[6]

But this was about to change. As the war ended, Smuts lost no time in raising anew the future of South-West

Africa, which had been run by South Africa as a Class C
Mandate since the ending of the First World War. In
June 1945, returning from San Francisco, he announced
that South Africa—rather than seeking to convert its administration into a UN trusteeship—would seek a formal termination of the mandate and the territory's full
incorporation within South Africa. The following January, this request was brought before the UN General Assembly at its first session in London. There the South
African delegate cautioned the assembly against rigidly
applying "theoretical principles of trusteeship" rather
than drawing on his country's long experience of governing natives. Africa "offers ... an almost virgin field
in which many of the mistakes and errors which have
clouded the economic and social development of more
advanced continents, such as Europe, can be avoided."
What that meant in particular was not rushing primitive
peoples to statehood faster than they could go. All that
the South Africans offered was a promise to consult the
local population of the mandate—the kind of offer that
would have made Stalin proud.[7]

Aware of the strength of feeling against the idea in
the United States, Smuts hoped for backing from the
British and indeed the Labor government agreed to support him. However this decision was not publicized,
and it was then complicated by a brilliantly effective
diplomatic campaign waged against the South Africans
by the experienced regent of Bechuanaland, Tshekedi
Khama. Khama had been approached by the leadership
of the African National Congress for help; but he also
had a direct interest of his own, for if South-West Africa

was annexed, he and his people and the other High Commission Territories within the borders of the Union of South Africa were likely to be next in line.

Thus for the first time in modern history, one African political leader lobbied internationally on behalf of another dependency, and it was the forum provided by the new world organization that made this possible. Smuts wanted Khama muzzled and prevented from coming to London, and threatened—this was the South African trump card—to take over the High Commission Territories by force if he did not get his way. As a result—for Whitehall was genuinely anxious about this happening and knew it could do nothing to stop it—the British refused to forward Khama's appeals to the UN and managed to prevent him from traveling. Frustrated, Khama openly questioned whether the "good faith of the nations" could be said to lie behind the new United Nations Organization when he was prevented from presenting his case to its assembly. Only in August did the Labor government finally come clean in public about its support for Smuts. Three months later, by the time the question of South-West Africa emerged at the General Assembly meeting in New York, Khama's lobbying had borne fruit, and the British found themselves embarrassingly isolated in their support for annexation. Aware of the sentiment against South Africa, Smuts backed away, proposing merely that the assembly should "take note" of the fact that South-West Africa's native inhabitants—according to him—wanted annexation. Even so, his motion was rejected by a large majority and South Africa was invited instead to propose a trusteeship arrangement to the General Assembly. As the historian of this minor but revealing affair has noted, Khama was "perhaps unique as the only African who had successfully opposed Smuts."[8]

Smuts's defeat over South-West Africa was an important marker of the changing climate of international opinion. Unlike in 1919, he actually enjoyed British backing for the idea of annexation; but this time British backing was no longer sufficient. Whitehall was not in the driver's seat, as it had been at the establishment of the League, and could not control the debate. The British tried to muzzle Khama, but he had resources at his disposal that had not been available earlier. International public opinion had hardened against any expansion of colonial rule—that very public opinion which Smuts himself had singled out in the preamble as so integral to the UN's eventual success. And that opinion could now be expressed by noncolonial powers acting within the General Assembly. Perhaps more important, it was exploited by the USSR as well and—anxious not to be outdone, at least in an areas of the world that they did not regard as strategically essential—by the Americans as well. The new world organization, unlike the old, thus had a potentially and sometimes actually anticolonial element in its directorate. In short, Smuts's annexationism was badly out of kilter with the times. It was one thing for the UN discreetly to connive in the preservation of the old empires; quite another, to allow them actually to *expand*, for this threatened to make a nonsense out of the Trusteeship scheme altogether.

And there was one power, in particular, on which Khama had relied, and whose role in the new international organization was becoming especially important, and that was India. It is likely that South Africa's request to annex South-West Africa would have been defeated in any case. What doomed it was the even more far-reaching debate that had preceded it in the assembly initiated by the Indian delegation on the subject of the plight of Indians in South Africa itself. This issue became the cause célèbre of the 1946 General Assembly and the pointer to a very different future.

ᔕ

Indians had first migrated to Southern Africa following the 1860 agreement between India and Natal for indentured laborers to work the coastal sugar plantations. From the start, they were a bone of contention between India and the colony, and twice India terminated the agreement. Legislation discriminating against Indians, chiefly in Natal, had long angered the Indian authorities but Whitehall and the South Africans were generally unmoved. As one British official put it at the start of the century, Whitehall would be bound to act similarly "if Natives of India showed any inclination to immigrate into this country." Writing after the end of the Boer War, in May 1903, Lord Milner justified the restrictive policy on segregationist grounds. "[It] is not directed against colour or against any special race," he claimed. "It is dictated by the necessity of preventing people of a higher degree of civilization, whatever their race or colour may be, from being degraded by enforced contact with people of lower grade." His acolytes drew the consequences for the future of their beloved Commonwealth: Indians in the Transvaal, wrote the young Lionel Curtis, archpriest of the commonwealth idea, should not be granted equal rights lest "in the coming centuries, the great reservoir of Indian races . . . be opened and allowed to deluge the whole of the Imperial Dominions."[9]

The issue also had a huge impact on the young Gandhi. He had arrived in 1894, set up the Natal Indian Congress, and organized his first political campaign of nonviolent resistance. There was thus an intimate relationship between the politicization of Indians in South Africa and the struggle for freedom in the Raj itself. When the 1913 anti-Indian Immigration Regulation Act was passed, Gandhi launched a second major campaign and won the act's modification. The problem resurfaced after the First World War with the growing standardization of racial segregation throughout South Africa, a policy which—as we have seen—was actually crafted by Smuts. During the imperial conferences of 1921–23, Smuts—even as he advanced his pioneering and influential blueprints for a modern British Commonwealth of Nations—rejected Indian government demands that Indians be given "all the rights of citizenship," fearing that this would lead to a general extension of the franchise and—from his perspective—the "end of South Africa." The fear articulated by Milner and Curtis—that mass migration might pollute the commonwealth itself—thus remained alive after the First World War. There were some in Britain—including Curtis's close colleague, Lord

Lothian—who did indeed believe that India should enter the Commonwealth. But when the British government passed the 1935 Government of India Act, it made it quite clear that India's role would be a subordinate one, without Dominion status and ruled by a governor general with far more sweeping powers than in the Dominions.[10]

Meanwhile, new segregationist legislation was continually applied to Indians in the Union throughout the interwar era (in the context, of course, of even more sweeping measures against Africans), and in 1939 the Transvaal Asiatic Land and Trading Act imposed a two-year ban on property transactions and the granting of licenses to Indians in Transvaal. Indian–South African relations had reached a low point by the time the war broke out. But during the war, they got even worse. White sentiment in Natal was strongly anti-Indian, and Smuts pandered to this on the eve of 1943 election by extending versions of the Transvaal measures—in the so-called "Pegging Act"—to Natal as well.

Indians were outraged and alleged that Smuts had broken his promise not to introduce discriminatory legislation during the war. At a meeting in Durban City Hall, one Indian protester tore up a copy of the Atlantic Charter, describing it as "first-class mockery," and the subsequent agitation brought Indian and African activists against white rule together for the first time. It was at this time that the Non-European Unity Movement was formed by a small group of Indian and African Marxists in an effort to unify the African and "Coloured" campaigns. News of the wartime measures was gleefully picked up by Axis propagandists. Berlin radio described the Pegging Act as the first installment of the Atlantic Charter, while Tokyo hailed it as a sign that the Europeans were squeezing Asians out of Africa and that Asia at least should be for the Asians. This, at any rate, was an alarming implication for British rule in India, and an Indian member of the Privy Council made the same point: the Pegging Act would dissolve the British Empire much sooner than any agitation in India itself because it would lead to the slogan of "Asia for the Asiatics." In what he described as "the Asiatic federation to come" there might be no place for Europeans.[11]

India's growing nationalism thus threw into relief the intrinsic conservatism of many of the leading Commonwealth theorists. Back in their early Kindergarten days in South Africa, Lionel Curtis had already decided that the Indians were incapable of self-government without a long period of tutelage. But the war was clearly telescoping this and bringing self-government much closer, and with hundreds of thousands of Indians fighting for the British, the Raj's new viceroy, Lord Wavell, felt obliged to take Indian complaints seriously. As these tensions within the imperial bureaucracy eroded imperial solidarity and heightened anticolonial feelings in India itself, Wavell warned Smuts that there would be reprisals for his policies. Indeed in July 1943, the Indian government passed an act (not immediately put into effect) allowing it to treat South Africans in India as Indians were being treated in South Africa. Economic sanctions were also considered and in November 1944, Wavell and his council actually applied the reciprocity act: it was a basically symbolic gesture and London was very unsympathetic, not surprisingly, since it feared open rupture within the Commonwealth during the war. Smuts himself was pessimistic: any solution satisfactory to Indians would outrage whites and vice versa. The Commonwealth on which he had set such store now risked coming apart. That conception, which as we have seen, offered British thinkers a powerful model for world order was apparently too rooted in the racial assumptions and hierarchies of the nineteenth century to serve the needs of the mid-twentieth.

~

It may be useful, at this point, to step back and take stock of the wider issues at stake in the Indian Ocean during the Second World War. In late 1940, a young South African Indian wrote Gandhi a letter that summed up the mixed feelings of many non-whites:

> I am puzzled as to what should be the attitude of Indians at the present juncture. The "White" races are so utterly callous in regard to "Coloured" people, and in spite of the war colour prejudice continues unabated. Why then should we give our lives for them? Quite recently an Indian student who returned here from Europe was telling us that in spite of the fact that the steamer was not crowded the British company hesitated to give accommodation to Indians. Such treatment leads us and also the African people to believe that there is no difference between the Nazis, the Boers and the British, so far as we are concerned. If there

were Nazi rule in South Africa, we could not be treated worse than we are today. Many of us think that the British are sweet-tongued but they pursue their own ruthless policy in spite of honeyed words, whereas Hitler would be more frank. He at any rate says exactly what he feels. Is there not truth in this?[12]

Gandhi's response was carefully worded. "There is not much to choose between the British and the Nazis," he wrote. "This is as clear as daylight in South Africa, in particular, where Coloured races are treated as definitely inferior in every way. What more than this could the Nazis say or do? The defeat of the British would connote the victory of the Nazis, which, again, we do not and must not desire. Therefore, we should be impartial. We are desirous of our own independence. For that there is no reason why we should want the destruction of Germany. We have to achieve as well as maintain our freedom through our own strength. We do not need British or any outside help for it."[13]

Viewed from Delhi, therefore, the fundamental question raised by the Second World War was not whether the British or the Germans would triumph but rather how non-Europeans might exploit the opportunities the European conflict offered to best smooth the path to independence. The immediate strategic problem was how and whether to choose between the opposing sides, a choice that was far from obvious. After all, the Axis powers proposed in 1940 to divide up the world into spheres of influence; but so did the Allies. As the *Bombay Chronicle* put it in 1943, following the

Teheran conference between the Big Three, "The design is clear: two worlds are being constructed—one the world of white and Imperialist 'Europe'—which includes America—and the other the world of its colored 'dependencies' of Asia and Africa." In short, what was bubbling up through the war was the deep dissatisfaction that had been growing since the start of the century throughout Asia in particular with the West's attitude to international governance in general and the hypocrisy of its universalist rhetoric in particular.[14]

Two recent studies have reminded us of the global disillusionment that followed the Wilsonian moment in 1919 and the anticolonial movements that subsequently emerged. Of these, Pan-Islamism and Pan-Arabism were in retrospect never as serious a threat as they seemed in the minds of British or Russian intelligence officers; they failed to gain backing from the new states of the Middle East—states which were, in any case, struggling to free themselves from British oversight in particular. The more serious challenge to European and American hegemony came from ideologies of Pan-Asianism, above all those emanating from Japan: this was the power—as it had been since 1905—that seemed best placed to challenge the international system's Western bias from within. In the 1920s, Japan gradually turned from Geneva, and broke emphatically with the League in 1931 when it invaded Manchuria. For the next fourteen years, and especially in the early 1940s, it was Japan that embodied the most muscular challenge to European rule, its claims to pan-Asian leadership resting uneasily on two bases—military domination and political emancipation (in theory if not practice). With the Japanese army's incursion into Southeast Asia, the potential appeal of Japan's slogan of "Asia for the Asians" alarmed Whitehall and the white settler Dominions even more. The New Zealand papers feared "the end of civilization as we have known it." Roosevelt's adviser, William Phillips, warned from India that "we have a vast bloc of Oriental peoples who have many things in common, including a growing dislike and distrust of the Occidental." In South Africa, Smuts himself wondered whether black Africans were not waiting for the Japanese to arrive and speculated on the consequences if India rose in revolt. One way to understand Smuts's hopes for the UN is as the instrument of a white man's alliance that could withstand— better than the Commonwealth now seemed able to do—the thrust of these other oppositional racial forces.[15]

For Indian nationalists in Delhi, therefore, the choice was not so much between Britain and Germany as between Britain and Japan. But in a sense, the Indian National Congress chose both. Deterred, as many in Congress had been, by Japanese militarism, Gandhi's preference, as outlined above, was for a conditional acceptance of British control. But to many others inside and outside the Congress movement such a stance seemed passive and indifferent to the opportunities presented by the war and the breach it had opened up in the European order. The most important exponent of this view, Subhas Chandra Bose, was expelled from Congress in 1940, and looked first to Nazi Germany for aid. Disappointed by Hitler's lukewarm support—his conversation with the Fuhrer in May 1942 made Hitler's caution very apparent—Bose turned his attention eastward. He denounced the strategy of "so-called United Nations" as a "poor imitation" of the Tripartite Pact (the wartime alliance between Fascist Italy, Germany and Japan) and warned that (as Churchill too insisted) the Atlantic Charter would not be applied to India. Even though public opinion in the United States sympathized with the cause of Indian independence, Bose noted the geopolitical ambition in Henry Luce's famous 1941 article hailing the coming "American Century" and insisted that the Roosevelt administration was dreaming of replacing the British Empire by their own supremacy in world affairs. The struggle for India thus logically required looking to "the enemies of the so-called United Nations."[16]

With Bose's arrival, the Japanese were therefore forced to think seriously about India. By common consent, the wartime Japanese Greater East Asian Co-Prosperity Sphere allocated only a marginal role to the country. But it did replicate the Atlantic Charter's rhetoric of respect for national sovereignty and international cooperation while providing an appealing and plausible critique of the Eurocentrism of the League and its successors. In November 1943, a conference called in Tokyo denounced British rule in the Raj and pledged its support for Bose. Had Japan won, Bose's Indian National Army would have freed India from the British and ushered in independence within a regional state system under Japanese hegemony. This prospect was enough to scare Roosevelt, who tried to get Churchill to make more concessions to Indian hopes. But Churchill stonewalled—he

and many British policymakers feared the Americans
nearly as much as the Japanese—and Bose, it turned
out, was betting on the wrong horse. In October 1943,
the Provisional Government of Free India, which he announced in Singapore, failed to win support from Congress. Not only was it evident by this time that Japan
faced defeat. As others in Congress were well aware,
even had the Japanese won, their victory would not
have guaranteed an important role for India in an Asian
system of states.[17]

For there was, within the upper echelons of the Congress movement, a very different conception of India's
place in the world, one best expressed in the many
speeches and writing on the issue by Jawaharlal Nehru—
Bose's rival at the top of the movement and Gandhi's
designated successor since 1942. Nehru had long called
for Indian nationalists to develop an internationalist
consciousness and prided himself on his interest in global developments. As early as 1928 he had advocated
a coalition of progressives, open to the USSR and its
"new civilization," an obstacle to "imperialism" and
helpful in extricating Indians from their "curious mentality of subservience to England, of the inevitability of
the British connection." "It was important to realize
that Britain was not all-powerful," he had argued, and
to understand that "the days of British dominion are
numbered." The rise of fascism in Europe merely added
urgency. Fascism was linked, for Nehru, to the problem of imperialism and exposed it for what it was; the
English, self-professed democrats, behaved like fascists
in India.[18]

Of course, fascism proper he recognized as a threat but even as it appeared to be triumphant, Nehru was demanding a revival of international cooperation. In the spring of 1939, shortly after the German march into Prague, he called for new efforts to succeed where the League of Nations had failed. For Nehru, the League had "started under wrong auspices. . . . It was an attempt to stabilize something which could not endure, to protect the imperialisms and special interests of the victor nations." In other words, a stable and enduring international body would by definition have to be anti-imperialist. But the idea that the League purportedly enshrined, the idea of collective peace based on freedom and democracy was one Nehru emphatically endorsed. More of a statist than Smuts, he wanted a "world union" in which autonomous national states would send representatives to a world union legislature that would extend the principles of a planned and socialized economy internationally. But the impracticality of this quickly struck him and less than a year later (perhaps influenced too by the realization that Indian independence was closer at hand than many had realized) he was writing instead of a world commonwealth of nations.[19]

One might almost say this was a Smutsian conception. Except that in the all-important details it was everything that Smuts condemned—a "wider commonwealth" that eschewed British or European leadership. Even though the proposed new United Nations as it emerged from the Big Four conversations at Dumbarton Oaks in 1944 was significantly different from what he was aiming at, Nehru could see its value. He understood the need to make sure the great powers supported it, and hence he supported allowing them a veto in the Security Council to prevent it sharing the fate of the League.[20] But this emphatically did not mean allowing it to retain the League's Eurocentrism, nor did it mean failing to exploit every avenue that existed to plead the anticolonial cause.

Opposing Eurocentrism meant above all asserting the power of Asia: this was something Nehru accepted as readily as the Japanese internationalists did. But for him it was India's job, not Japan's, to do this. How to secure India's leadership role within the region was a subject he had been concerned with since the Russo-Japanese war and had written about in his 1932 *Asia's Response to the Call of the New Age*. There he argued that Asia must not respond to Europe's power by imitation but by giving the new age "a voice in its own idiom of civilization." Asianism, which in Bose's strategy implied freeing India under the flag of Japanese leadership, for Nehru was best achieved by working within the new British-American-Soviet condominium.

Japan's defeat bankrupted the Bose strategy and cleared the way for Nehru. Once the war was over, he lost no time combating European moves to restore colonial control. As early as December 1945 he proposed an Asian conference to promote regional cooperation; three months later, after a tour of Southeast Asia, and all too aware of British efforts to shore up French and Dutch rule in the region, he repeated the call. "The whole system known as colonialism has to go," he told the *New York Times* in March 1946. "It is evident that the dependent peoples of the colonial empires are in a rebellious mood, and cannot be suppressed for long, and every attempt to suppress them is a drain on the ruling country which weakens it. . . . One decadent empire tries to help another still more ramshackle empire and in this process speeds up the process of its own dissolution." How to move on? "The first big step," he concluded, "is a clear renunciation of colonialism and imperialism. . . . within the larger framework of the world order that is slowly evolving." He clearly felt that the San Francisco conference the previous spring had failed in this regard.[21]

Once installed at the head of the Interim government in the run-up to Indian independence, he turned to the United Nations Organization. Contemplating whether or not to demand a place in its Security Council, Nehru noted that India was "potentially a Great Power"—the center of a future security system in Asia and the Indian Ocean; "it is absurd for India to be treated like any small power." Whatever happened with the Security Council, India's "natural position" was as leader of "all the smaller countries of Asia." Thus when an astonishingly ill-timed new piece of South African anti-Indian legislation—the 1946 Asiatic Land Tenure and Indian Representation Act galvanized Indian sentiment by its proposals to restrict their voting and residence rights—Nehru seized on the issue to push his wider agenda. It would put India in the vanguard of the movement to challenge colonial domination, and it would increase the pressure to stop applying different principles to different parts of the world. Above all, "there is no reason why Europe and the Americas should be considered the pivots of the modern world and Asia should be ignored. Asia is inevitably going to be one of the big centers of international affairs in the future and the sooner this is recognized and given effect, the better." India's foreign policy, he told the press at the end of September, revolved around "the ending of colonialism all over Asia or for that matter in Africa or elsewhere, and racial equality . . . and the ending of domination or exploitation of one nation by another." By this time, the struggle for the soul of the UN was well under way.[22]

⤺

It was as though everything happened in 1946. At the start of that year, as the first UN General Assembly met in London, and tensions between South Africa and India rose, the Indian High Commissioner in South Africa was brought home for consultations, carrying with him Smuts's outline of a new bill. Behind the scenes, the viceroy, Wavell, had asked Smuts to hold it up, but this had had no effect. The proposed new bill came as a shock to Indian public opinion since Indians would be given the vote but only as second-class citizens—subject to educational and property qualification—and residence restrictions would create Indian "ghettoes."

Indian politicians wanted London to do something. But Whitehall had no desire to intervene since it had no answer to the deadlock and regarded the problem as one "for India and S[outh] Africa alone."[23] It was a critical moment for the Commonwealth. Since the 1920s it had been moving toward the idea that member-states should *not* take disputes between them before international bodies. On the other hand, although Commonwealth cohesion implied some kind of arbitration procedures among members, in fact no formal such mechanisms existed, especially since India's very status within the organization was as yet indeterminate. British civil servants in London sounded astonishingly feeble. They wished that Nehru had not made "the rather empty gesture" of taking the South Africa issue to the UN and that they could have avoided "this washing of family linen." But they were paralyzed, not wanting to take sides between two valued members of the empire, and regarded Nehru's move fatalistically. As Wavell pointed out, even if an intra-Commonwealth mechanism had existed, Nehru would probably not have used it because he regarded other Commonwealth states as racially prejudiced as well.[24]

In short, race politics—and Smuts's own policies—were causing his beloved Commonwealth to seize up: white settler rule, it turned out, could not be demarcated so easily from Britain's other colonial interests and that "moral community" that the Commonwealth was supposed to embody turned out to be a sham. (One might add indeed that this process was also visible in the way Canada, Australia, and New Zealand came out of the war increasingly dependent strategically on the United States: by the late 1940s, the term *dominions* was already falling into disuse).[25] News of Nehru's move triggered a revealing discussion back in London about whether an independent India should be invited to remain in the Commonwealth at all. Would it not risk "weakening the cohesion of the Anglo-Saxon club as we know it"? Fed up with the Indians, one civil servant believed that they were trying to create an "Asiatic bloc" against Britain and the United States, and thought that if they stayed inside the Commonwealth, they would simply behave like "a more irritating Ireland." Yet India remained, at least for the military and the navy, the lynchpin of postwar British imperial strategy. The best policy for London was thus to keep out of the quarrel altogether. Imperial control was breaking down as a result of the empire's own internal contradictions, which had been magnified in an increasingly democratic age. The India Office urged Britain's own UN delegation to observe the most scrupulous neutrality in the upcoming debate so as not to push independent India into the arms of the Russians.[26]

It was the Natal Indian Congress that had set the ball rolling when it reacted to news of the proposed new South African law by urging Delhi to help and suggesting that the Indian Government raise the issue at the UN. In the Indian capital, Dr. Narayan Khare, the member of the viceroy's council responsible for Indians overseas, was at first pessimistic about the chances of success but took the suggestion up. It was, so he later recollected, not an uncontroversial move: "One of my colleagues said to my face that an ICS [Indian Civil Service man] would never have behaved irresponsibly like that . . . the Viceroy charged me with irresponsibility."[27] Inside India's external affairs department, the civil servants discussed whether such a move was even possible. Concluding that it was, they advised Khare to raise the question in the General Assembly rather than before the Security Council (since it was not a threat to world peace). The South African side was bound to argue that it was a matter of domestic jurisdiction and would probably win; on the other hand, perhaps India could itself draw on the language of moral responsibility and say that it had an obligation to look after Indians in South Africa until they enjoyed full civic rights.

A senior civil servant in India's external affairs department advised thinking the thing through properly and not dismissing the domestic jurisdiction objection too quickly: what, after all, about "a later stage if there are dissatisfied minorities in the country and they secure support from some not too friendly disposed country for their case to be placed before the UNO"? (It was at precisely this time that British lawyers were weighing up whether to include a minorities' protection clause in the draft treaty granting Indian independence). But the risk was dismissed as unimportant—no one in Congress appears to have taken minority rights protection seriously any more—and the arguments for going to the UN (which were *not* to be made on minority rights grounds) regarded as overwhelming. After all, it was claimed, South Africa would want to present "a most spotless appearance" in order to succeed with its own application to annex South-West Africa. In this way, India hoped to take advantage of Khama's complaint just as he wanted to take advantage of theirs.[28] Despite the fact that the issue had not been raised either with the British India Office or with the members of the cabinet mission who had arrived in India in

March, the viceroy raised minimal objections and London's discouraging telegrams that returned in response were simply ignored, since they did no more than rehearse considerations that had already been considered in Delhi.[29]

In June 1946 the South African Asiatic Land Tenure and Representation Act came into force and a much-publicized civil disobedience campaign was launched in Natal and Transvaal. Two weeks later, the viceroy's council finally decided to appeal to the General Assembly and the complaint was officially lodged at the end of June. To the annoyance of its sponsor Dr. Khare, however, who had been expelled from the Congress Party in 1938 and was none too fond of it, it was the Congress-led Interim Government, with Nehru as its head and acting foreign affairs minister, that came into office that September, that would take the credit. South Africa was the first issue Nehru raised with Wavell. And Gandhi, in consultation with the viceroy decided to send a strong Indian delegation to the UN General Assembly meeting in New York, headed by Nehru's formidable sister, Vijaya Lakshmi Pandit. Both Gandhi and Nehru were determined — in Nehru's words—to make the UNO dissociate itself from South Africa and cut the latter away from the family of nations if it followed "the Nazi doctrine." And Nehru added a warning to the UN's sponsors: if the UNO, Europe, or America did not do this then "the time will soon come when all Asia may do that and so might Africa."[30]

Despite the long history of South African–Indian bitterness over the issue, it is nevertheless understandable that Smuts was taken aback by the Indian initiative. In the first place, the question of preventing the new world body meddling in the internal affairs of its members—the so-called domestic jurisdiction issue—had been extensively discussed at the San Francisco conference not least by Commonwealth leaders. No state had an interest in allowing the UN to intervene in matters of domestic policy—not the United States, sensitive about civil rights in the South, nor the Soviet Union, nor indeed the British Empire. Dominion leaders had helped shaped the contentious Article 2:7 of the Charter (the domestic jurisdiction reservation) precisely in order to preclude such issues being brought before the UN; but they had been backed not only by the United States but also by many South American countries who feared larger powers using the UN to interfere in their internal affairs. Smuts himself had demanded assurances that the South African Indian question was not admissible and had informed his parliament accordingly. Nor had the then Indian government objected. Barely a year later, however, it was behaving very differently, denouncing a fellow-member of the Commonwealth, drawing—infuriatingly on Smuts's own rhetorical "faith in basic human rights"—and all that before it had even achieved independence.[31]

As for the British, they were appalled: the Indian initiative represented "a radical blow to the very conception of the Empire." Once British theorists had envisaged a world security organization as a kind of adjunct to their empire; now the new United Nations seemed to threaten its existence, But in fact they had even more alarming worries: what, for instance, if they lost their grip over the Raj altogether and the new world body ended up discussing not only South Africa, but India too. Strange as it may now seem, in the feverish negotiations that stretched through 1946 over the future of the subcontinent, the British cabinet was haunted by the fear that if they failed to reach a settlement, the *whole* Indian question might end up being referred to the UN. For Palestine was one thing, the Raj quite another, and the cabinet disliked the very idea of letting the UN get involved. Ernest Bevin, the foreign secretary, warned this would amount to "handing over the Empire of India to the Soviet Union" since that was "the only country ready and able to supply the numbers of troops the situation would require." Congress's approval would clearly be required for such a move, and thus Nehru's decision to go to the UN over the South African issue was, among other things, a reminder to the British that they were no longer the sole arbiters even of India's destiny, let alone that of the empire as a whole.[32]

In the autumn of 1946, Gandhi and an increasingly exhausted Nehru instructed their delegation that they "should try to stay clear of rival power blocs and try to ease the tensions that such blocs generated." That September Nehru publicized his view that this was not "merely an Indian issue" but rather "a world cause" that concerned Asians, Africans, and all those struggling for "equality of opportunity for all races and against the Nazi doctrine of racialism." The basic parameters of his postwar internationalism were already evident: neutrality in any Cold War polarization between the great powers, together with advocacy not merely for some putative

"Asia" but for colonial peoples across the globe, offered the best chance for India to exercise leadership.[33]

↪

At the General Assembly meeting itself in December, the reception of the Indian complaint revealed several surprising features of the new world order. One was the willingness of the assembly to hear it at all. Although Smuts warned that it turned minorities once again into an object of international concern—an issue which, as we saw in the previous chapter, the UN as a whole had seemed happy to relegate to the past—almost no other delegation seemed worried at the precedent. (With perfect logic, if little tact, Smuts's Nationalist opponents back home would later threaten to treat the Indians as the East Europeans had treated their minorities, by expelling them.) Between the wars, it was international law that had supposedly safeguarded minorities through the League. But the assembly showed a marked impatience with the idea of allowing law to determine policy. The United States, Britain, South Africa, and the other Commonwealth states wanted the International Court of Justice to test India's claim that the South African treatment of Indians was incompatible with their UN Charter obligations. The Canadians spoke of upholding respect for international law; the British warned that the assembly was not yet "a world parliament." But the Indians claimed that this was too important a matter to be left to the lawyers and many others agreed. The Soviet delegation rejected the legal route, saying taking this would minimize the political importance of the issue and weaken the prestige of the United Nations itself. The anticolonial thrust of this critique was inescapable: noting that the colonial powers were now in a permanent minority in the General Assembly, the British deplored "the general attitude of mind" there that "the possession of colonies is in itself something reprehensible." But the whole point of the Indian complaint was to allege that racial prejudice threatened peace. The strict reading of the domestic jurisdiction clause was set aside; legal niceties were ignored, and in yet another sign of the waning power of international law, the letter of the Charter was trumped by the spirit of human rights and moral anger, ironically precisely those forces that Smuts himself had invoked eighteen months earlier. Smuts, as it were, had defeated himself.[34]

Thus the Indian motion was voted through the committees and, with some modifications, eventually squeaked through the assembly as well (by 32 to 15 with 7 abstentions) and Mrs. Pandit, the head of the Indian delegation, claimed an "Asian victory." She famously made her way over to Smuts and asked his forgiveness if she should have failed to match the high standard of behavior set by Gandhi. "You have won a hollow victory," Smuts is said to have told her. "This vote will put me out of power in our next elections but you will have gained nothing."[35]

The Indian delegation was jubilant and telegrams of congratulation poured in. Nehru enthused that the General Assembly had "not only vindicated India's honour but has shown itself a guardian of human rights. This is full of hope for the future of the United Nations Organisation and for civilization." Privately, he also welcomed the fact that this had demonstrated that Indians were not just "camp-followers of the British"; the Interim government had thus already changed how the world viewed India. Now, identified with an independent foreign policy, it could rightfully claim a role as leaders in Asia and mediate between the colonial powers and those Asians—in Burma, French Indochina, and Indonesia—struggling for their freedom. Japan was occupied, the Chinese were subservient to the Americans. Nehru's studied neutrality in the U.S.–USSR standoff simply underscored India's new prominence. (And it had the side benefit of drawing attention away from the violence sweeping India itself.)[36]

Smuts's reaction was very different. He too discerned the emergence of an Asian system of powers, but for him this spelled the imminent end of European civilization and confirmed the grim feeling that had possessed him since the end of the war, when the sight of the great powers deadlocked gave him the sense of being stranded in an epoch "of transition." In Java, the Dutch were "in dire trouble," he wrote a friend in November 1945, "the English in India; both were likely to be "booted out in spite of the magnificent work they have done. . . . it reminds me of what must have been the experience of the Britons in England after they had wiped the Romans out and their conditions reverted to the prior barbarism. But of course people prefer to govern themselves badly rather than be well governed by others." To Wavell, the viceroy of India, he wrote in December with foreboding that India's determination to "go her own way" could bring down "the whole vast system" of the empire; a breakup could lead to partition and set the subcontinent back "to where it was before the British Raj ... first united the sub-continent. In fact all Asia seems to be on the move to get rid of its European guides and it may wander in the dark into dangerous paths. And beyond that lies the issue of East and West and all it may mean for our human future." In short, decolonization, by destroying that unifying global force which had been European civilization threatened mankind with new dangers of fragmentation, barbarism, and perhaps—though Smuts rarely spelled this out—race war.[37]

Some such thinking underpinned his attitude on the Indian question in South Africa. Smuts felt that "the European with all his faults carries a message for Africa which India does not." In the summer of 1946 he already anticipated a frosty reception in New York but he does not seem to have expected the wholesale repudiation he received there. In Paris for the peace conference, that September, he pinned his hopes on the tens of thousands of Europeans—mostly refugees—who wanted to leave the Old Continent for South Africa; the Afrikaners would complain but this was "our chance if we want more whites to augment our small numbers." According to this reasoning, a substantial influx of Europeans offered the only possible means to relax segregationism at home. When he learned that India would take its case against South Africa to the UNO, he attributed it to Nehru's desire to divert attention from his own troubles at home, and he anticipated lining up once more against

Gandhi, as he had half a century earlier. By the end of September he realized there was "heavy weather" ahead in New York.[38]

Once there, he ruminated on what the opposition implied. "South Africa, "he wrote, "is a little epic of European civilization on a dark continent." It was this "noble experiment" that was being threatened by India and its "vast millions," invading the country and "penetrating in all sorts of devious ways to reverse the role which we have thought our destiny." The stakes could not have been higher, according to him. "East and West meet there at this moment of history and I frankly am a Westerner, although I love and respect the whole human family, irrespective of colour or race. We stand for something which will go and be lost to the world, if India gets control of eastern South Africa." This was, in short, nothing less than a global war between civilization and barbarism, and South Africa was on the front line. For Smuts, the irony was bitter. There he was trying to avoid pogroms and racial bitterness, being accused of racism by a government whose country was at that moment in the throes of communal violence the likes of which South Africa had never witnessed. Were events in India not in fact an argument for segregation? Yet he seemed to be the only one capable of seeing things that way. Even his beloved British Commonwealth was coming under fire at the UNO as a system of "mere exploitation of other, inferior peoples." His own mission to the UN had been a "failure." His defeat at the hands of India had inflamed tempers and left people in South Africa "dazed and amazed." He himself had been "exposed as a hypocrite and a double-faced time server," and even the natives had been stirred up by "all this talk of equality and non-discrimination," as he knew from his own servants and farm workers. His sole consolation, but it was scarcely that, was that he saw everything in grand historical terms: Europe was being booted out of Asia and the Far East. "Some vast change is coming over the course of history" while Europe itself was prostrated by the war. "The world is reeling between the two poles of White and Colour"; it was "today in a precarious and dangerous position such as has not existed since the fall of Rome." Not only could the UNO not lead it out; it appeared to have become part of the problem.[39]

~

And there was precious little comfort for him in the General Assembly's deliberations on the same subject the following year. The South African case was as poorly put and as poorly received as ever. Smuts himself stood accused of having made disparaging remarks about the UN back home, and of undermining his own creation, the international postwar commitment to human rights. Smuts might have helped draw up the UN Charter, asserted the Polish delegate, "but the policy of [his government] is in direct contradiction to [its] noble ideals." As for Smuts's invocation of the domestic jurisdiction clause, "the Polish people reject this fascist idea which reminds us so closely of the German *Herrenvolk*. Racial discrimination leads to expansionism and war." West European delegates were more sympathetic to the idea of asking

the International Court of Justice to decide on the ad-
missibility of the issue, but the majority once again took
the view that the legal issue was secondary: UN prestige
would be jeopardized if it allowed a clear case of state-
sanctioned racial discrimination to stand. As the Yugo-
slav delegate, a former partisan, put it: the "similarity
between the Hitlerite frame of mind, and that of the authorities and even it appears of the parliament of a
member nation of the United Nations is striking." Even
those delegates—and there were many—with warm
words to say about Smuts lined up to criticize his government. As for the United States, it sat uncomfortably
on the fence, talking up the need for an international
bill of rights, supporting the legalist option, and suggesting a conference to talk the issue out.[40]

But as the year before, it was the Indian delegate, the
quick-witted and eloquent Vijaya Lakshmi Pandit, who
stole the show. She pointed out the failure to act on the
previous year's resolution—negotiations between India
and South Africa had failed to materialize—and warned
that the latter's position had global implications. "Those
of us who believed in the creation of a new world order
cannot but view with anxiety the danger of a growing
disharmony between races—that way lies conflict and
ultimate disaster." The problem was the South African
claim that segregation was the "best road to racial harmony." The issue was not one of national minorities and
their rights but "the arrogance and racial pride of the
European community." Against this, the South African's
claim that his country's policy was not about racial superiority, but simply differences of development, rang

hollow. This time round, India failed to reach the necessary two-thirds majority. But its delegates were undeterred and the UN General Assembly returned annually to the subject of South Africa for more than a decade. A moral victory had been won by Delhi.[41]

⤳

The emergence in the General Assembly of an entirely new conception of world order—one premised on the breakup of empire rather than its continuation, on politics rather than law—was no figment of the imagination. The General Assembly itself had proved more unpredictable than the drafters of the UN Charter had anticipated. And, for a time, it was more powerful too. As the emergent Cold War increasingly paralyzed the Security Council, business shifted to the General Assembly. The General Assembly debated Franco's regime in Spain, partitioned Palestine, and adjudicated trusteeship disputes more forcefully than the League had done. It was vocal on decolonization struggles in the Maghreb and Africa in particular. By September 1948, British foreign secretary Ernest Bevin was reduced to deploring—to the third assembly meeting in Paris—the "misguided and false idea that the possession of Colonies is bad in itself."[42] Every act of decolonization swelled the size of the assembly and diluted the strength of Europe's voice. With the great wave of accessions in 1960—a year when sixteen new states won independence and membership—the Afro-Asian bloc was worth 46 out of 99 votes. The continent that had enjoyed the smallest representation in 1946 had the most numerous grouping of states less than two decades later.[43]

But the faster this new, anticolonial assembly grew, the less it was able to do. After Smuts fell from power, a new hard-line Nationalist government set about building an apartheid state in South Africa. Indians were never actually expelled en masse. But in 1950 they were defined under the Group Areas Act as having a "national home" in South Asia; their voting rights were removed, and in 1955 they were struck from the common electoral roll in the Cape. India and Pakistan regularly joined forces to complain to the UN, and General Assembly votes went equally regularly against South Africa. But none of this had any effect. In 1961 the Nationalists took South Africa out of the Commonwealth, destroying the last vestiges of inter-Commonwealth solidarity. Even the United Nations was divided and the pressure emanating from the assembly was blunted by the toleration extended by Security Council members—notably the United States and the United Kingdom—toward the apartheid regime. When the Security Council itself discussed the situation there for the first time—in the aftermath of the 1960 Sharpeville massacre—both Britain and France abstained from a vote calling on the government to abandon apartheid.

The South African government's idea of winning support was to warn the West of the grim racial balance of power. In ten years time, its delegate told the council, there would be thirty-seven Western white nations to fifty African-Asians, and twelve communist states. "It is not only South Africa, but every Western nation that is faced with the question of what its position will be in 1970." The interesting thing is how poorly this kind of language played; compared with the fearful atmosphere of the 1920s, the 1960s were singularly unconcerned about the prospects of global race war, or of some kind of clash between "the West" and "East." Experience had shown people what percipient observers had known all along—that "Asia" was a figment of propagandists' imaginations, as divided internally as Europe if not more. Insofar as there was a "West," it was directed not against a racially defined Orient but against the ideological enemy, Soviet communism. The fault lines of the global Cold War ran through continents, not across them. And both sides valued their participation in the UN too much to exit it.[44]

Nehru's Asianism thus turned out to be a dead end. Indian support for independence struggles in Indochina and Indonesia was real. But Asianism's high point in its Indian incarnation was probably the Inter-Asian Relations conference in March 1947. There Nehru hailed the centrality of "Asian civilisation" and looked forward to the departure of the British, because—so he said—they had cut India off from the rest of Asia whereas in reality it was a "vital bridge." But the "new Asia" he invited the assembled delegates to build never materialized. Nehru claimed to project Asia to the world; and the rapturous receptions he received in Vietnam and China in the 1950s suggest that the message went down well among some of India's neighbors. But the Bandung conference of 1955 showed that in fact Asia was deeply divided by the Cold War—Nehru's hope of rising above its tensions was unrealizable—and the war with China in 1962 marked an end, perhaps temporary, to the old talk of "Asian values." As he put it in 1955, "To talk about [Asia] as one entity is to confuse ourselves" and "to talk of Europe and Asia and America as separate entities is also misleading, for the future at any rate. "[45]

India's UN strategy, however, blazed a path others would follow, for the General Assembly had proven itself as a forum for publicity, if little more. And publicity could work too (as believers in the international mind like Woodrow Wilson and Zimmern had always claimed). Even though the UN had been established by the great powers, Third World nationalists took its universalist rhetoric at face value, exploited its mechanisms, and fostered international public opposition to continued colonial rule. Anticolonialism provided the cause within which the weakest part of the UN found itself—the cause which non-European peoples could exploit most effectively. When India defeated the Portuguese and annexed Goa (on the grounds that the Portuguese as the colonial power had no real claim to sovereignty), the General Assembly's approval showed how far internationalism had come from the heyday of empire: at the start of the twentieth century, it had been the colonial powers that would determine and recognize sovereignty; now their very status as colonial powers rendered those claims suspect. Yet in the process, Western norms of sovereignty and statehood had been universalized, and a genuinely "international society" of states of the kind analyzed by postwar political scientists came into being for the first time.[46] Asian states won independence and joined; Africa did the same. Even the Cold War failed to prevent UN growth, and after Stalin's death, the United States and the USSR finally agreed to allow in each other's client states—fascist Spain and Portugal on the one hand, communist satellites on the other. It was as though the logic that Smuts had outlined—the idea of a commonwealth of nations respectful of sovereignty while acknowledging the primacy of great powers —still held. But this was no commonwealth as he had conceived it, neither in its attitude to race, nor in its lack of moral or spiritual unity. Indeed, the price paid for this globalization of membership was a high one—an excessive deference to the sovereignty of member states, an inability to live up to the UN's own professed ideals, a sharp and growing gulf between the Security Council and the General Assembly— in short, increasing marginalization from world events. Former colonial possessions, once independent, tried to keep the UN out of their affairs as hard as they had once tried dragging it into those of their imperial masters. Collective security, once the primary motivation for international organization, was left to regional pacts and constellations of powers that gravitated around the two superpowers. The Cold War offered an alibi for impotence. But once it came to an end, and the spotlight was trained on the UN once more, the resuscitation of the old ideals soon exposed them for what they were— dreams of a past that had never existed and a poor guide to what might lie ahead.

§ Afterword

The point upon which attention needs to be focused for the serious student of international affairs is that the United Nations does not represent
a break with the past, but rather the continued
application of old ideas and methods with some
changes deemed necessary in the light of past experience. If people would only recognize this simple truth, they might be more intelligent in their
evaluation of past efforts and more tolerant in the
appraisal of present efforts.

— L. Goodrich, "From League of Nations to United Nations," *International Organization* 1:1 (Feb. 1947), 5

Could the UN return to the ideals of its founders even if
it wanted to? Only by ignoring both the important ways
in which the world has changed since their day and the
ambiguous and indeed contradictory nature of those
ideals themselves. Which founders, after all? Cynics
highlight the 1944 Dumbarton Oaks conversations
among Americans, British, and Russian policymakers to
support their view that the UN was set up to be nothing
more than a tool of the great powers. Optimists, on the
other hand, emphasize the ambitious moral language of

the Charter and its preamble. And as we have seen, while some of the UN's inspirers and architects sought to preserve European colonial rule, others foresaw its demise. In short, it is not so much that the hopes of the UN's founders were derailed during the Cold War but rather that those hopes—ambiguous and often mutually contradictory—were not exactly what we imagine them to have been, nor as decisive in shaping the UN as we might think. We should thus not be disappointed that the UN so often fails to carry out the goals its founding rhetoric lays out; rather we should be curious about how, despite functioning as the product of the historical and political forces outlined here, it has managed on occasions to rise above them and redefine itself in the face of new and unforeseen circumstances. Its flexibility over time and its capacity for reinvention are without question as remarkable as its shortcomings.

⌒

Long before the UN's emergence—and before the drafting of the Charter—there lay a variety of ways of thinking about international cooperation that valorized the idea of establishing a world body of some kind. The desire to protect and promote human rights was among them but it was certainly not the most important of these. Much more significant, what I have called the imperial internationalism of the early twentieth century sought to reconcile the interests of the British Empire with the preservation of its civilizational mission. Redefining constitutional associations among its component parts would help to prop up an empire in decline and offer a new way to project its self-defined sense of moral purpose globally. Above all, it might reconcile the empire with the emergence of settler colonial nationalism, head off the danger of disintegration, and cement the imperial defenses against future threats.

The League of Nations, from Whitehall's pragmatic perspective, was thus an imperial project that looked as if it could simultaneously cement the alliance with the United States, shore up Eastern Europe against Bolshevism, and link Britain's European and imperial commitments. Yet the League itself was merely one possible incarnation of the idea of world community and indeed not as persuasive a model (for many inter-war British commentators) as the commonwealth concept from which it was derived. According to its propagandists, the Commonwealth presented a more cohesive and organic unity than the League precisely because of the solidarity and interdependence among its members and the longer imperial history behind it. Others agreed. "The British Empire can be seen as a League of Nations within the League of Nations," wrote the Japanese colonial theorist, Yanaihara Tadao, in the 1920s, "a more solid unity of nations than the League of Nations. Each Dominion has its autonomy as a nation and the British Empire is not supposed to have colonial domination over any of them." This was basically Smuts's vision, and Zimmern's too, and the model—in their minds—for a world organization as well.[1]

Yet the racial limits of the commonwealth idea were also limits to their conception of the global community in the making. For the foreseeable future, any granting of independence to African and Asian peoples was regarded as irresponsible and likely to lead to chaos. National self-determination was basically for Europeans. Iraq was the only League mandate granted independence between the wars, and that—ironically—because Whitehall had decided that British imperial interests would better be served by a nominal independence than by hanging on to an expensive mandate. In general, it was felt to be obvious that national self-determination was not for everyone. Thus a British civil servant in the Colonial Office worried in 1943 that the end of the war might bring independence to the colonies and thereby "a great multiplication of small national sovereignties. . . . This idea is disastrous," he continued. "It is at least arguable that we are suffering at the moment from too *much* independence and too little interdependence."[2]

The European crisis not only struck a deathblow to the commonwealth idea; it highlighted even more starkly the deficiencies of the League of Nations as well. The latter's inability to defend the Versailles settlement bankrupted it and brought to an end Europe's—and in particular Britain's—control of world affairs. Hastening the fall of European colonial empires, the war appeared to provide the most graphic and bloody reminder that people and nations could achieve protection and international recognition only through states of their own, not through minority rights. Nazism also corroded the idea of a common civilization expressing itself in legal norms that European international lawyers had developed in the previous century. (That conception would henceforth underpin the development of new exclusively European intergovernmental organizations and conventions.) In many ways the war marked a nadir in the influence of this profession, a blow to the lawyers' confidence that they could offer effective adjudication of disputes between states.

What emerged in 1945 at San Francisco was the League reborn, only now modified and adjusted— thanks to the Big Three conversations at Dumbarton Oaks—to the frank realities of a new configuration of great power politics. Like the League, the United Nations was, much more than a mere alliance, an international organization with global aspirations; like the League, it spoke for humanity but acted through national governments. Like the League it talked about international law but deliberately avoided turning rhetoric into substance. But this time round, both the commitment to national self-determination and the turn away from law were more extensive. Tension and ambiguity were thus hardwired into the UN from the start. It promised more about rights than the League, but did less about them. It gave more power to the permanent members of the Security Council but opened its doors to a much larger cohort of new, independent states than the League had done. The result was both weakness and flexibility, allowing the new world body to shed one skin after another in response to the changing climate of international affairs.

The League had been an instrument of empire and it had offered a basically imperial conception of world governance in which leadership would be provided by the mature statecraft of the great powers, with newcomers brought in when they were deemed "civilized." Underpinning its deliberations was a sense of normative solidarity and, never far from the surface, a pronounced sense of global hierarchy. Men like Smuts were haunted by fears of global race war—they talked in a strange vocabulary of White against Black or Brown or Yellow—and of anti-Western movements such as Pan-Africanism, Pan-Asianism and Pan-Islam. These fears largely disappeared after 1945, and did so for a reason. Fearing minorities more than the League had done, the UN was also more welcoming to nationalisms, seeing the small nations who made up many of its original members as one of the principal victims of fascism. Outside as well as inside Europe, partition not minority rights was the new path to international peace, or so it was thought. There was no "standard of civilization" to be applied, no intervention in the affairs of newcomers. This readiness to recognize independence movements across the colonial world reflected not the powers' confidence in the civilizing potential of their modernization theories and development techniques, but rather the collapse of Europe in the aftermath of the war and the need generated by American perceptions of the Cold War to undercut the appeal of communism globally and to provide an alternative leadership for anticolonialism. Smuts was taken by surprise as early as 1946 by the UN's willingness to disregard its own Charter, with the General Assembly overriding the domestic jurisdiction clause to castigate his country's racial policies. But he should have been prepared: a world body governed as the UN was not by formal law but by the appeal to morality and world conscience was bound to be shaped by fluctuations in the climate of values and norms and more than usually willing to rewrite its own rules.

The rise of an anti-imperial UN was not instantaneous, of course. On the contrary, despite the Indian victory in 1946, the initial sense of many of the UN's principal backers was that it might still serve the old purposes. British prime minister Ernest Bevin, speaking in January 1948, saw the UN Charter as enabling Western Europe to recover by drawing on the resources of colonial Africa. As he put it, referring to the Soviet veto, if one could get round "this ideological thing that is constantly coming up," the UN should still be able to live up to expectations and act as a great power concert, as it had done against the Nazis. Where the powers were able to reach agreement—over Israel, for example, or the former Italian colonies in Africa—the UN was able to act decisively. But in most cases this proved impossible. The Cold War paralyzed the Security Council, and by making Big Three agreement all but impossible, it doomed it—and thus the UN itself—to impotence on the larger questions of war and peace. Instead, regional organizations like NATO arose to provide collective security, or (as in the Council of Europe) to defend human rights. What was left for the UN by the late 1940s was, on the one hand, the development of the technical agencies for economic and social global transformation, and on the other, the instauration in the General Assembly of the world's postcolonial order.[3]

The General Assembly's members were keen to assert their political role and in 1950, briefly, this brought a new kind of interest from Washington. Realists like George Kennan might scorn "the whole idea of world peace"; President Truman himself might question—as he did in 1947—the UN's ability to protect American security. Yet it was with the encouragement of the United States that the assembly met much more frequently than the Council, taking the lead on issues such as trusteeships and the plight of colonial peoples in general. Washington put together the Uniting for Peace resolution, which a few years later provided the authorization for Secretary-General Dag Hammarskjöld to raise the profile of his office and embark on a new area of UN activity—peacekeeping—in the aftermath of the Suez crisis. The UN Military Staff might have proved abortive; likewise the attempt to use the UN to get atomic weapons under international control; but in this more modest area of international life, the world body quickly proved its utility.[4]

Still, a politicized General Assembly was not a reliable instrument for American goals. Majority voting gave as much power to small states as to large ones and the outcomes were too unpredictable for Washington. Soon Smuts's discomfort was followed by Washington's. Zimmern's old student, the American secretary of state Dean Rusk, who had been such an ardent enthusiast for the UN at the time of the Korean War, had lost faith in its usefulness by the time of Vietnam. After him there was no American diplomat of any consequence who seriously believed that the UN could play a central role in promoting U.S. foreign policy. Unwavering U.S. support of Israel after the occupation of the West Bank also played its part, driving a wedge between Washington and the prevailing mood in the General Assembly, which was increasingly sympathetic to the idea that the Palestinian fight for national self-determination itself represented a stage in the struggle against European colonialism. In the Reagan years, the UN was denounced as "anti-American," and the U.S. ambassador to the UN warned against unquestioning compliance with the Charter's prohibitions against the use of force.[5]

In truth, the UN was never a plausible instrument of ideological warfare. Its relaxed criteria for entry were designed to encourage universality of membership precisely in order to avoid the creation of international factions and rival alliances outside the world body. Thus the sole criterion for membership was deliberately established as an external one—the fact of a state's "peace-loving" nature. Eventually Franco's Spain was admitted (there was a similar earlier argument over Argentina) and apartheid South Africa was never expelled. This may have blunted the organization's ability to shape global moral or political norms but also allowed it to endure, to adapt to rapid shifts in international politics, and to offer enemies the chance to meet and talk. The major expansion of membership in 1955 showed that this desire was shared across the Iron Curtain.[6]

Decolonization accentuated this heterogeneity and thus created a third UN. As the Cold War began, and the United States became *the* dominant global power and turned into a new kind of empire, with far-flung bases and numerous client states, the world body was being transformed as well. With its enormous expansion of membership between 1955 and 1965, the General Assembly turned from critic of the old colonial status quo to defender of a new global order of nation-states. It was one more, largely unexpected, change of identity—and one that once again led to a mismatch between power and appearance. The UN could now claim more persuasively than ever before to speak for the peoples of the world, but in some ways it could do less than ever for them. Scholars talked of the emergence of a genuinely "international society" of states. But the smallest members of the UN today guard their sovereignty as jealously as the great powers did in the long nineteenth century and erect systemic barriers to intervention by would-be humanitarian interventionists. As early as 1961, an American political scientist noted that "there is more nationalism than internationalism manifested today."[7]

Hence the present impasse. The UN's foundational rhetoric appeals to the idea of a morality superior to reason of state. Successfully mystified, believers in and detractors of the UN both talk about its sad loss of moral purpose, and seek either to restore it or to find it elsewhere. But both groups mistake rhetoric for reality and misunderstand what the UN has been, and still more, has been able to become. What the UN's present member-states have in common is basically a shared acceptance of diplomatic and legal norms regarding the recognition and mutual interaction of states. They find these too useful to give up—there has been only one instance of a member voluntarily withdrawing from the

UN (Indonesia in 1965) and that lasted less than a year—but the notion of moral community that Zimmern and other theorists had argued necessarily bound members of a common civilization no longer exists. The force of international public opinion is real, if often opaque or fragmentary; but the determination of member-states to resist intervention in their affairs is as strong if not stronger than ever. In effect, both the legalist and the moralist versions of international organization conceived as the alternatives facing the world on the eve of the First World War have, a century later, been defeated by the global triumph of the sovereign state.

Yet while sovereignty has become ever more strongly entrenched in the UN, other globalization processes over the past forty years—vast flows of liquidity, migrants, arms, and greenhouse gases—all make a mockery of the idea of sovereign independence. And in recent years, there has been a different kind of challenge as the emergence of a new humanitarianism has prompted calls for the UN to intervene decisively in its members' internal affairs in defense of the so-called "responsibility to protect." Its proponents argue that this is necessary to uphold the Genocide Convention, and more generally, to prevent states carrying out mass violations of human rights with impunity. But the politics of history cannot be ignored or swept aside quite as easily as the new humanitarians would like. Humanitarianism likes to see itself in terms of pure virtue, a kind of antipolitical gesture of compassionate brotherhood. But it is generally the same states that once, as imperial powers, intervened across the globe in the name of freedom that now lead the charge against the human rights abuses and the "organised hypocrisy" of the sovereignty claimed by many new and shaky states. Forgetful of their colonial past, Western states see in their liberalism only the benign face of a universal aspiration. Yet the states they target are generally those that have emerged recently from out of the rubble of those empires, and the critique of "failed states," couched in the comfortingly humanitarian language of our times, can sound uncomfortably like the old civilizational arrogance of Jan Smuts's generation. In fact, the old questions that haunted the minority rights regime of the League of Nations have not gone away. Who will decide when to intervene and where the right to protect shall be applied? Will it really be universal? Will it be extended beyond Africa—to the Gaza strip for example, or Colombia, or northeastern India? A world of sovereign states may lead to political leaders committing crimes against their own people, but intervention is a political and military act with numerous potential drawbacks too, as Afghanistan readily demonstrates.

It is exceptionally easy to write the story of the UN as failure. It failed in its original incarnation—helping liberal empires spread their values, and with them civilization—around the world, because this could not withstand the collapse of empire that followed Hitler's demise. (It is no coincidence that the commonwealth idea, so closely connected to its origins, fared still worse; its history has been one of "continuous disintegration.")[8] And it failed in its second incarnation—as great power alliance that would police world peace—because that

presupposed a continuation of the wartime alliance between the United States, Britain, and the Soviet Union.
The erosion of that unity meant that the UN could only
function as a great power directorate in a negative sense:
it could not do what individual powers wanted if others
opposed them, but it could prevent things happening
against their will. The result was that the UN had only
the most marginal impact on security in Europe and by
extension elsewhere.

Yet what is more striking, if less generally remarked
on, is that unlike its predecessor, to which it otherwise
owes so much, the UN has not been shackled by such
failures. The League of Nations, umbilically tied to the
European peace settlement, died with the rise of the
Nazis. But responsibility for the defense of the post-
1945 European settlement could not be laid at the door
of the UN, and anyway, in a fundamental sense, the division of Germany *was* the basis of the peace. Marginal-
ity may have brought survival, just as ambiguity in its
founding Charter and activism from within the organization has brought flexibility and adaptation. As it is,
the UN has already lasted more than three times as long
as the League. It has inserted itself into international life
through the organization of peacekeeping—a function
unforeseen by the Charter—and via the vast expansion
of the technical agencies that it inherited from the
League. Between them, these now form a crucial part of
the ecology of modern global politics even though by
themselves they hardly put the UN back at the center of
the international system. Recent claims that wholesale
reform will engineer a sweeping transformation of the

UN's role in world affairs thus need to be viewed with caution. There may be many good reasons for reform. But calls for the UN to engineer a revolution in international law, in human rights enforcement, or in democratic values are probably doomed to fail, and if the UN's role in coordinating draconian anti-terror legislation after 9/11 is any guide, this may be for the best. The past is emphatically not destiny and the UN's origins need not shape its future. But without some knowledge of the context from which it emerged, we are likely simply to continue rehearsing the arguments of the past rather than to move successfully beyond them.

Notes ∫

INTRODUCTION

1. B. Boutros-Ghali, "Empowering the United Nations," Foreign Affairs 71:6 (winter 1992–93): 89–102; cf. B. Russett and J. S. Sutterlin, "The UN in a New World Order," Foreign Affairs 70:2 (spring 1991): 69–83; "An Agenda for Peace: Preventive Diplomacy, Peacemaking, and Peace-keeping," Report of the Secretary-General Pursuant to the Statement Adopted by the Summit Meeting of the Security Council on 31 January 1992, UN document A/47/277 - S/24111, 17 June 1992.

2. For an insightful critical analysis of the entire reform debate, see Hans-Martin Jaeger, "UN Reform, Biopolitics, and Global Governmentality," unpublished paper. My thanks to Professor Jaeger for allowing me to see this.

3. For one of the starting points, see G. John Ikenberry and Anne-Marie Slaughter, *Forging a World of Liberty under the Law: U.S. National Security in the 21st Century, Final Report of the Princeton Project on National Security* (Princeton, 2006), which included a draft "Charter for a Concert of Democracies." The literature on a democratic peace begins with Michael Doyle, "Kant, Liberal Legacies, and Foreign Affairs," *Philosophy and Public Affairs* 12:3 (summer 1983): 205–35; and 12:4 (October 1983): 325–53. See, too, Doyle, "Three Pillars of the Liberal Peace," *American Political Science Review* 99:3 (August 2005): 463–66.

4. Michael J. Glennon, "Why the Security Council Failed," *Foreign Affairs* 82:3 (May/June 2003); A. Grigorescu, "Mapping the UN-League of Nations Analogy: Are There Still Lessons to Be Learned from the League?" *Global Governance* 11 (2005): 25–42.

5. cf. Akira Iriye, *Global Community: The Role of International Organizations in the Making of the Modern World* (California, 2002).

For a pithy if partial historicization of the concept of internationalism, see P. Anderson, "Internationalism: A Breviary," *New Left Review* 14 (Mar.–Apr. 2002).

6. Two outstanding exceptions are R. Hilderbrand, *Dumbarton Oaks: The Origins of the United Nations and the Search for Postwar Security* (Chapel Hill, 1990), and B. Urquhart, *Ralph Bunche: An American Life* (New York, 1993). A new wave of historical interest is presaged by: S. Amrith and G. Sluga, "New Histories of the United Nations," *Journal of World History* 19:3 (Sept. 2008): 251–74 and the subsequent articles in that volume.

7. J. Winter, *Dreams of Peace and Freedom: Utopian Moments in the 20th Century* (New Haven, 2006), 1. Among the works in this vein are S. Schlesinger, *Act of Creation: The Founding of the United Nations* (New York, 2003); M. A. Glendon, *A World Made New: Eleanor Roosevelt and the Universal Declaration of Human Rights* (New York, 2001); E. Borgwardt, *A New Deal for the World: America's Vision for Human Rights* (Cambridge, MA, 2005); Paul Kennedy, *The Parliament of Man: The Past, Present, and Future of the United Nations* (New York, 2006); Samantha Power, *A Problem from Hell: America and the Age of Genocide* (New York, 2002); J. Cooper, *Raphael Lemkin and the Struggle for the Genocide Convention* (London, 2008). The UN Intellectual History Project has led to the publication of nine volumes, of varying quality: perhaps the best are J. Toye and R. Toye, eds., *The UN and Global Political Economy: Trade, Finance, and Development* (Indiana, 2004); and R. Normand and S. Zaidi, eds., *Human Rights at the UN: The Political History of Universal Justice* (Indiana, 2008).

8. P. A. Reynolds and E. J. Hughes, eds., *The Historian as Diplomat: Charles Kingsley Webster and the United Nations, 1939–1946* (London, 1976), 69–71; K. Sellars, *The Rise and Rise of Human Rights* (Stroud, Gloucestershire, UK, 2002), 8–10.

9. Samuel Moyn, "On the Genealogy of Morals," *The Nation* (16 April 2007); A. Brian Simpson, *Human Rights and the End of Empire: Britain and the Genesis of the European Convention* (Oxford, 2001); M. Mazower, "The Strange Triumph of Human Rights: 1933–1950," *Historical Journal* 47:2 (2004): 379–98. The history of human rights movements in the 20th century also formed the subject of a conference held in 2008 at the Social Science Research Center, Berlin: a report is available online at http://hsozkult.geschichte.hu-berlin

.de/tagungsberichte/id=2208&count=122&recno=8&sort=datum&
order=down&geschichte=79.

10. For a recent scathing critique from within the field, see R. N.
LeBow, *A Cultural Theory of International Relations* (Cambridge,
2008), which offers a pointed analysis of these shortcoming before
posing an alternative highly idiosyncratic framework based on permanent cultural and psychological values first supposedly articulated by the ancient Greeks. This theory seems much less useful than
the critique: those outside IR may feel it demonstrates that the real
problem is looking for "theories" in this area the first place. For
those wishing to explore the still underresearched history of American social science after 1945, P. Mirowski, *Machine Dreams: Economics Becomes a Cyborg Science* (Cambridge, 2002) is indispensable. See, too, D. Green and J. Shapiro, *Pathologies of Rational
Choice Theory: A Critique of Applications in Political Science* (New
Haven, CT, 1994).

11. N. Guilhot, "The Realist Gambit: Postwar American Political
Science and the Birth of IR Theory," *International Political Sociol-
ogy* 2:4 (Dec. 2008): 281–304; Kennan's comments in G. Kennan,
Memoirs, 1925–1950 (New York, 1967), 229–32; also J. G. Ruggie,
*Constructing the World Polity: Essays on International Institution-
alization* (London, 1998), 212–13; cf. Perry Anderson, "Our Man,"
(a review of James Traub, *The Best of Intentions: Kofi Annan and
the UN in the Era of American World Power*, and S. Meisler, *Kofi
Annan: A Man of Peace in a World of War*) *London Review of
Books* (10 May 2007). For insightful comments on the analytical
problems, see J. G. Ruggie, *Constructing the World Polity: Essays on
International Institutionalization* (London, 1998); P. Wilson, "The
Twenty Years' Crisis and the Category of 'Idealism' in International
Relations," in *Thinkers of the Twenty Years' Crisis: Interwar Idealism Revisited,* ed. Long and Wilson (Oxford, 1995), 1–25. One
would not, of course, want to ignore the role of political scientists
such as Inis Claude in analyzing international institutions in the
early postwar decades. But their impact on international relations
theory was slight.

12. G. John Ikenberry, *After Victory: Institutions, Strategic Re-
straint, and the Rebuilding of Order after Major Wars* (Princeton,
2001), and his *Liberal Order and Imperial Ambition* (London, 2006).
Doubts about the UN are articulated, for instance in Ikenberry and

Slaughter, *Forging a World of Liberty*. Slaughter is the author of "The Real New World Order," *Foreign Affairs* 76: 5 (Sept–Oct. 1997): 183–98, and the argument is extended in her *A New World Order* (Princeton, 2004).

13. Ikenberry, "Illusions of Empire: Defining the New American Order," *Foreign Affairs* 83:2 (Mar.–Apr. 2004):144–55. A critique of the intellectual genealogy of democratic peace theory may be found in B. Jahn, "Classical Smoke, Classical Mirror: Kant and Mill in Liberal International Relations Theory," in *Classical Theory in International Relations*, ed. Jahn (Cambridge, 2006), 178–207. On the single path to modernity, see D. Deudney and G. John Ikenberry, "The Myth of the Autocratic Revival: Why Liberal Democracy Will Prevail," *Foreign Affairs* 88:1 (Jan/Feb 2009): 77–94. On the compatibility of multilateralism and democracy, see R. Keohane, S. Macedo, and A. Moravcsik, "Democracy-enhancing Multilateralism," *International Organization* 63 (winter 2009): 1–31.

14. G. John Ikenberry, T. J. Knock, A.-M. Slaughter, and T. Smith, *The Crisis of American Foreign Policy: Wilsonianism in the Twenty-First Century* (Princeton, 2009).

15. Cf. A. Smith, *America's Mission: The United States and the Worldwide Struggle for Democracy* (Princeton, 1994), chapters 1–4; E. Manela, *The Wilsonian Moment: Self-Determination and the International Origins of Anticolonial Nationalism* (Oxford, 2007) charts the rise and rapid fall of global confidence in Wilson and his message.

16. C. Eichelberger, *Organizing for Peace* (London, 1977). Andrew Williams, *Failed Imagination? New World Orders of the Twentieth Century* (Manchester, 1998), 96 (Dulles), 130–31 on the Chatham House group, 189–91 on the State Department; Reynolds and Hughes, eds., *Historian as Diplomat*, 28–29. D. C. Watts has remarked on the continuities between the British planners in 1918–19 and 1939–45: D. C. Watt, "Every War Must End: Wartime Planning for Postwar Security in Britain and America in the Wars of 1914–1918 and 1939–1945: The Role of Historical Example and of Professional Historians," *Transactions of the Royal Historical Society* 28 (1978): 159–73; N. Mansergh, *Survey of British Commonwealth Affairs* (Oxford, 1958), 308. Churchill's lack of support, combined with a basically pro-League attitude, is analyzed in E. J. Hughes, "Winston

Churchill and the Formation of the United Nations Organization," *Journal of Contemporary History* 9:4 (Oct. 1974): 177–94.

17. *New York Times* cited by R. Divine, *Second Chance: The Triumph of Internationalism in America during World War II* (New York, 1971), 228.

18. Ruth B. Russell, *A History of the United Nations Charter: The Role of the United States, 1940–1945* (Washington, DC, 1958), 195; M. Hankey, *Diplomacy by Conference: Studies in Public Affairs, 1920–1946* (London, 1946), 121. In general, see A. Grigorescu, "Mapping the UN–League of Nations Analogy: Are There Still Lessons to Be Learned from the League?" *Global Governance* 11 (2005): 25–42.

19. Russell, *History of the UN Charter*; H. Notter, *Postwar Foreign Policy Preparation, 1939–1945* (Washington, 1949).

20. W.E.B. DuBois, "Prospects of a World without Race Conflict," *American Journal of Sociology* 49:5 (March 1944): 450.

21. Stimson cited in Williams, *Failed Imagination?* 84.

22. V. Pavone, *From the Labyrinth of the World to the Paradise of the Heart: Science and Humanism in UNESCO's Approach to Globalization* (Lanham, MD, 2008), 71–72.

23. Reynolds and Hughes, eds., *Historian as Diplomat*, 68.

24. See H. McKinnon Wood, "Notes on the Question of Domestic Jurisdiction under the Charter of the United Nations," *British Documents on Foreign Affairs*, series IV: M:2 (1946) (Bethesda, MD, 2002), 281–83.

CHAPTER 1

JAN SMUTS AND IMPERIAL INTERNATIONALISM

1. *Documents of the UN Conference on International Organisation* (London, 1945), I, 420–26.

2. J. A. Hobson, "The Scientific Basis of Imperialism," *Political Science Quarterly* 17:3 (Sept. 1902): 489; D. Bell, "Democracy and Empire: Hobson, Hobhouse, and the Crisis of Liberalism," in *British International Thinkers from Thomas Hobbes to Lewis Namier*, ed. Ian Hall and Lisa Hill (Basingstoke, UK, 2009).

3. For the older movement, see Duncan J. Bell, *The Idea of Greater Britain: Empire and the Future of World Order, 1860–1900* (Cambridge, 2008).

4. S. Dubow, "Colonial Nationalism, the Milner Kindergarten, and the Rise of South Africanism, 1902–1910," *History Workshop Journal* 43 (1997): 53–85. See for background, J. E. Kendle, *The Round Table and Imperial Union* (Toronto, 1975), and W. Nimocks, *Milner's Young Men: The "Kindergarten" in Edwardian Imperial Affairs* (Durham, NC, 1968).

5. M. Lake and H. Reynolds, *Drawing the Global Colour Line: White Men's Countries and the International Challenge of Racial Equality* (Cambridge, 2008).

6. J. Smuts, *Wartime Speeches: A Compilation of Public Utterances in Great Britain* (New York, 1917), vi.

7. W. K. Hancock, *Smuts: The Sanguine Years, 1870–1919* (Cambridge, 1962), 1:198.

8. P. Anker, *Imperial Ecology: Environmental Order in the British Empire, 1895–1945* (Cambridge, MA:, 2001), 46–47; Hancock, *Smuts: Sanguine Years*, 1:428–31; W. K. Hancock and J. van der Poel, eds., *Selections from the Smuts Papers* (Cambridge, 1973), 5:111.

9. Hancock, *Sanguine Years*, 1:431–38, 500.

10. Ibid., 1:467.

11. Ibid., 1:501.

12. G. W. Egerton, *Great Britain and the Creation of the League of Nations* (Chapel Hill, 1978), 421.

13. On Woolf, see Peter Wilson, *The International Theory of Leonard Woolf: A Study in Twentieth-Century Idealism* (Basingstoke, UK, 2003), chaps. 3–4.

14. J. Smuts, *The League of Nations: A Practical Suggestion* (London, 1918); P. Yearwood, "'On the Safe and Right Lines': The Lloyd George Government and the Origins of the League of Nations, 1916–1918," *Historical Journal* 32:1 (March 1989): 131–55, 151.

15. G. Egerton, *Great Britain and the Creation of the League of Nations* (Chapel Hill, NC, 1978), 103–7; P. Raffo, "The Anglo-American Preliminary Negotiations for a League of Nations," *Journal of Contemporary History*, 9:4 (Oct. 1974): 153–76.

16. George Curry, "Woodrow Wilson, Jan Smuts, and the Versailles Settlement," *American Historical Review* 66:4 (July 1961): 968–86.

17. The standard work is T. Knock, *To End All Wars: Woodrow Wilson and the Quest for a New World Order* (Oxford, 1992).

18. V. Rothwell, *British War Aims and Peace Diplomacy, 1914–1918* (Oxford, 1971), 212.

19. Egerton, *Great Britain and the Creation*, 118; cf. Knock, *To End All Wars*, 201–7.

20. Kendle, *Round Table*, 256–57; W. Roger Louis, "The Repartition of Africa" and "The United States and the Colonial Settlement of 1919," reprinted in Roger Louis, *Ends of British Imperialism* (London, 2006), 205–25, 225–51; Knock, *To End All Wars*, 214–16.

21. E. Haas, "The Reconciliation of Conflicting Colonial Policy Aims: Acceptance of the League of Nations Mandate System," *International Organization* 6:4 (Nov. 1952): 321–36.

22. Louis, "Repartition of Africa," 208.

23. Louis, *Ends of British Imperialism*, 198–99; Hancock, *Sanguine Years*, 1:507.

24. Smuts, *Wartime Speeches* (New York, 1917), 75.

25. Ibid., 77.

26. W. K. Hancock, *Smuts: The Fields of Force, 1919–1950* (Cambridge, 1968), 2:56–57.

27. L. Stoddard, *The Rising Tide of Color against White World Supremacy* (New York, 1922), 1–6.

28. Ibid., 89; on Stoddard's Asian readers, see Aydin, *The Politics of Anti-Westernism in Asia* (New York, 2007), 150.

29. R. Hyam, *The Failure of South African Expansion, 1908–1948* (New York, 1972), chap.1; Louis, *Ends of British Imperialism*, 109; Hancock, *Sanguine Years*, 1:223, 189.

30. T.H.R. Davenport, *South Africa: A Modern History* (London, 1977), 233–35, 252–53; Hancock, *Fields of Force*, 2:117; Robert M. Maxon, "The Devonshire Declaration: The Myth of Missionary Intervention," *History in Africa* 18 (1991): 259–71; S. Dubow, *Racial Segregation and the Origins of Apartheid in South Africa, 1919–1936* (London, 1989), 4.

31. Hancock, *Sanguine Years*, 1:284; Hancock and van der Poel, eds., *Smuts Papers*, 5:35.

32. Donald Birn, *The League of Nations Union, 1918–1945* (Oxford, 1981), 123.

33. Anker, *Imperial Ecology*; J. Morefield, *Covenants without Swords: Idealist Liberalism and the Spirit of Empire* (Princeton, NJ, 2005), chap. 3; Hancock and van der Poel, eds., *Smuts Papers*, 5:439.

34. Hancock and van der Poel, eds., *Smuts Papers*, 5:511.

35. W. Roger Louis, *Imperialism at Bay: The United States and the Decolonization of the British Empire, 1941–1945* (Oxford, 1978), 318; Hyam, *Failure of South African Expansion*, 198.

36. Hyam, *Failure of South African Expansion*, 191.

37. Hancock, *Sanguine Years*, 1:371; Hancock and van der Poel, eds., *Smuts Papers*, 6:331–43.

38. Hancock and van der Poel, eds., *Smuts Papers*, 6:456–69; S. Gish, *Alfred B. Xuma: African, American, South African* (New York, 2000), 121–27; Louis, *Imperialism at Bay*, 106, 172, 219, 337–42.

39. J. Smuts, *Toward a Better World* (New York, 1944), 233, 245; Hancock and van der Poel, eds., *Smuts Papers* (Dec. 1934–August 1945), 6:269–74.

40. A good firsthand discussion is in Clark Eichelberger, *Organizing for Peace: A Personal History of the Founding of the United Nations* (London, 1977). On federation, see in this regard R. Hillmann, "Quincy Wright and the Commission to Study the Organisation of the Peace," *Global Governance* 4:4 (Oct–Dec 1998); on Amery, see C. Brewin, "Arnold Toynbee, Chatham House, and Research in a Global Context," in *Thinkers of the Twenty Years' Crisis: Interwar Idealism Revisited*, ed. D. Long and P. Wilson (Oxford, 1991), 291.

41. R. C. Hilderbrand, *Dumbarton Oaks: The Origins of the United Nations and the Search for Postwar Security* (Chapel Hill, NC, 1990), 226–27; general account in R. H. Russell, *A History of the United Nations Charter: The Role of the United States, 1940–1945* (Washington, DC, 1958); Churchill in E. J. Hughes, "Winston Churchill and the Formation of the United Nations Organization," *Journal of Contemporary History* 9:4 (Oct. 1974): 190.

42. Russell, *History*, 43.

43. P. A. Reynolds and E. J. Hughes, *The Historian as Diplomat: Charles Kingsley Webster and the United Nations, 1939–1946* (London, 1976), 57.

44. T. Hoopes and D. Brinkley, *FDR and the Creation of the United Nations* (New Haven, CT, 1997), 204.

45. H. Aptheker, ed., *Correspondence of W.E.B. DuBois: Selections, 1944–1963* (Amherst, MA, 1997), 24–25, 39.

46. *Documents of the UNCIO* (New York, 1945), 1:233–34, 710–11; M. Sherwood, "There is No New Deal for the Blackman in

San Francisco: African Attempts to Influence the Founding Conference of the United Nations, April–June 1945," *International Journal
of African Historical Studies*, 29:1 (1996): 90–93; on the UN and
colonies, see Russell, *History*, 808–24. R. Normand and S. Zaidi,
eds., *Human Rights at the UN: The Political History of Universal
Justice* (Indiana, 2008), 127–35; also P. Orders, "Adjusting to a New
Period in World History: Franklin Roosevelt and European Colonialism," and V. Pungong, "The US and the International Trusteeship
System," in *The US and Decolonisation*, ed. M. Ryan and V. Pungong (New York, 2000), 63–84, 85–101.

47. Reynolds and Hughes, *Historian as Diplomat*, 69–71.

48. S. Dubow, "Smuts, the United Nations and the Rhetoric of
Race and Rights," *Journal of Contemporary History* 43:1 (2008):
43–72, esp. 56–57.

49. W. K. Hancock, *Sanguine Years*, 1:55–56; for background, see
Louis, *Imperialism at Bay*, chap. 34.

CHAPTER 2
ALFRED ZIMMERN AND THE EMPIRE OF FREEDOM

1. On Zimmern, see D. J. Markwell, "Sir Alfred Zimmern Revisited: Fifty Years On," *Review of International Studies* 12 (1986):
279–92; J. Morefield, *Covenants without Swords: Idealist Imperialism and the Spirit of Empire* (Princeton, 2005); P. Rich, "Alfred
Zimmern's Cautious Idealism: The League of Nations, International Education and the Commonwealth," in *Thinkers of the
Twenty Years' Crisis: Interwar Idealism Reconsidered*, ed. D. Long
and P. Wilson (Oxford, 1995), 79–100. Polly Low, *Interstate Relations in Classical Greece: Morality and Power* (Cambridge, 2007),
has some useful reflections as does Frank Trentmann, "After the
Nation-State: Citizenship, Empire, and Global Coordination in the
New Internationalism, 1914–1930," in *Beyond Sovereignty: Britain,
Empire and Transnationalism, c1880–1950*, ed. K. Grant, P. Levine,
and F. Trentmann (New York, 2007), 34–54.

2. A. Zimmern, *The Greek Commonwealth: Politics and Economics in Fifth Century Athens* (New York, 1961 [1911]), 19–20; see
too J. Stapleton, "Gilbert Murray and Alfred Eckhard Zimmern," in
*Gilbert Murray Reassessed: Hellenism, Theatre, and International
Politics*, ed. C. Stray (Oxford, 2007), 261–93.

3. *Greek Commonwealth*, 191–96.

4. A good discussion in the excellent J. Morefield, *Covenants without Swords*, 68–73; for the background, Sandra M. Den Otter, *British Idealism and Social Explanation* (Oxford, 1996); and Frank Turner, *The Greek Heritage in Victorian Britain* (New Haven, 1981), 366–67. M. Richter, *The Politics of Conscience: T. H. Green and His Age* (Cambridge, MA, 1964). Cf J. H. Muirhead, in his *Chapters from Aristotle's Ethics* (Oxford, 1900): "The good of the individual ought never to be separated from the good of the whole of which he is a part—ethics from politics."

5. Cited in R. L. Nettleship, *Memoir of Thomas Hill Green* (London, 1906), 238. See too D. Bell and C. Sylvest, "International Society in Victorian Political Thought: T. H. Green, Herbert Spencer, and Henry Sidgwick," *Modern Intellectual History* 3:2 (2006): 207–38.

6. John A. Hobson, *Imperialism, A Study* (London, 1902), chap.4; for transformations in Oxford attitudes to empire, see R. Symonds, *Oxford and Empire: The Last Lost Cause?* (Basingstoke, 1986).

7. G. Murray, "The Exploitation of Inferior Races in Ancient and Modern Times," in *Liberalism and the Empire*, ed. F. Hirst, G. Murray, and J. L. Hammond (London, 1900), 118–57.

8. D. Gorman, "Lionel Curtis, Imperial Citizenship, and the Quest for Unity," *The Historian* 66 (2004): 67–96.

9. cf. J. E. Kendle, *The Round Table and Imperial Union* (Toronto, 1975), 171–73. A subtle and detailed analysis is provided in Jeanne Morefield, "'An Education to Greece': The Round Table, Imperial Theory and the Uses of History," *History of Political Thought* 28:2 (2007): 328–61.

10. Stray, ed., *Gilbert Murray*, 12–13; Peter Wilson, *The International Theory of Leonard Woolf: A Study in Twentieth-Century Idealism* (Basingstoke, UK, 2003), 44–51.

11. G. K. Peatling, "Globalism, Hegemonism, and British Power: J. A. Hobson and Alfred Zimmern Reconsidered," *History* 89:295 (2004): 381–98; Morefield, *Covenants without Sword*, 145–46; Kendle, *Round Table Movement*, 224–27 (on India).

12. Kendle, *Round Table*, 253; A. Zimmern, *Nationality and Government* (New York, 1918), 355.

13. Knock, *To End All Wars*, 3. My thanks to Stephen Wertheim for sharing his ideas with me.

14. Cf. A. Sharp, "Some Relevant Historians—The Political Intelligence Department of the Foreign Office, 1918–1920," *Australian Journal of Politics and History* 34:3 (1989): 359–68.

15. A. Zimmern, *The League of Nations and the Rule of Law, 1918–1935* (London, 1936), 160–78.

16. Re. Zimmern's essays in *Nationality and Government* (New York, 1918).

17. Ibid., 193–211.

18. Kendle, *Round Table*, 255.

19. Wells's ideas in J. S. Partington, *Building Cosmopolis: The Political Thought of H. G. Wells* (London, 2003).

20. P. Yearwood, "'On the Safe and Right Lines': The Lloyd George Government and the Origins of the League of Nations, 1916–1918," *Historical Journal* 32:1 (March 1989): 131–55; P. Rich, "Alfred Zimmern's Cautious Idealism," in *Thinkers of the Twenty Years' Crisis*, 79–100.

21. Kendle, *Round Table*, 256.

22. Peatling, "Globalism, Hegemonism, and British Power," 391 (Zimmern-Hobson, 29 Sept. 1916).

23. Stapleton, "Gilbert Murray and Alfred Eckhard Zimmern," 281.

24. A. Zimmern, *Europe in Convalescence* (New York, 1922), 214–19.

25. A .Oslander, "Rereading Early Twentieth-Century IR Theory: Idealism Revisited," *International Studies Quarterly* 42:3 (1998): 419.

26. A. Zimmern, *The League of Nations and the Rule of Law, 1918–1935* (London, 1936), 278.

27. J. Darwin, "A Third British Empire? The Dominion Idea in Imperial Politics," *Oxford History of the British Empire* (Oxford, 1998), 69–72.

28. A. Zimmern, *The Third British Empire: Being a Course of Lecture Delivered at Columbia University, New York* (London, 1926).

29. Ibid., 60–92.

30. J. Coatman, review of Zimmern, *The Third British Empire*, 3d ed. (1934), *International Affairs* 14:3 (May–June 1935), 419–20.

31. Oslander, "Rereading Early Twentieth-Century IR Theory," 409–32.

32. I. Parmar, "Anglo-American Elites in the Interwar Years: Idealism and Power in the Intellectual Roots of Chatham House and the Council on Foreign Relations," *International Relations* 16: 1

(Apr. 2002), 53–75; see, for an example of this educational work, A. Zimmern, ed., *University Teaching of International Relations: A Record of the Eleventh Session of the International Studies Conference, Prague 1938* (Paris, 1939).

33. P. Wilson, "The Myth of the First Great Debate," *Review of International Studies* 24:5 (1998): 1–15; J. Quirk and D. Vigneswaran, "The Construction of an Edifice: The Story of a First Great Debate," *Review of International Studies* (2005) 31: 89–107; R. Rich, "Reinventing Peace: David Davies, Alfred Zimmern, and Liberal Internationalism in Interwar Britain," *International Relations* 16 (2002): 117–33.

34. H. De Capello, "The Creation of the United Nations Educational, Scientific, and Cultural Organization," *International Organization* 24:1 (winter 1970): 1–30; F. R. Cowell, "Planning the Organization of UNESCO, 1942–1946: A Personal Record," *Journal of World History* 10 (1966): 210–56.

35. A. Zimmern, "Athens and America," *Classical Journal* 43:1 (Oct. 1947): 3–11; Zimmern, "Our Greek Augustan Age," *Classical Journal* 46:7 (Apr. 1951): 325–54; Zimmern, *The America Road to World Peace* (New York, 1953).

36. Quirk and Vigneswaran, "The Construction of an Edifice."

37. For some preliminary thoughts on this see M. Mazower, "'An International Civilization'? Empire, Internationalism, and the Crisis of the Mid-20th Century," *International Affairs* 82: 3 (2006): 553–66; and Mazower, "Paved Intentions: Civilization and Imperialism," *World Affairs* (fall 2008).

38. T. E. Zeiler, *Dean Rusk: Defending the American Mission Abroad* (Wilmington, 2000), 26–27; Paul Rich, "Alfred Zimmern's Cautious Internationalism: The League of Nations, International Education, and the Commonwealth," *Thinkers of the Twenty Years' Crisis*, 79–100.

39. John Henry II and William Espinosa, "The Tragedy of Dean Rusk," *Foreign Policy* 8 (autumn 1972): 166–89.

40. Zimmern, "Athens and America"; Zimmern, *American Road to World Peace* (New York, 1953), 241.

41. Cited in Morefield, *Covenants without Swords*, 225, and see too her article, "Empire, Tragedy, and the Liberal State in the Writings of Niall Ferguson and Michael Ignatieff," *Theory and Event* 11:3 (2008).

42. A.-M.Slaughter, "America's Edge: Power in the Networked Century," *Foreign Affairs* (Jan–Feb. 2009).

CHAPTER 3
NATIONS, REFUGEES, AND TERRITORY

1. M. Levene, "Nationalism and its Alternatives in the International Arena: The Jewish Question at Paris, 1919," *Journal of Contemporary History* 28 (1993): 511–31; and Levene, *War, Jews, and the New Europe: The Diplomacy of Lucien Wolf, 1914–1919* (Oxford, 1992); the classic study is I. Claude, *National Minorities: An International Problem* (Cambridge, MA, 1955).

2. L. Holborn, "The Legal Status of Political Refugees, 1920–1938," *American Journal of International Law* 32:4 (Oct. 1938): 680–703; C. Skran, *Refugees in Interwar Europe: The Emergence of a Regime* (Oxford, 1995).

3. Leading a shadow existence during the war, the IGC would play a role in the formation of the postwar International Refugee Organization: "Intergovernmental Committee on Refugees," *International Organization* 1:1 (Feb. 1947): 144–45.

4. N. Smith, *American Empire: Roosevelt's Geographer and the Prelude to Globalization* (California, 2004), 295–56; R. Medoff, *Zionism and the Arabs: An American Jewish Dilemma, 1898–1948* (London, 1997), 85. See too, A. Bashford, "Population, Geopolitics and International Organizations in the Mid Twentieth Century," *Journal of World History* 19:3 (Sept. 2008): 327–48.

5. Henry Field, *"M" Project for FDR: Studies in Migration and Settlement* (Ann Arbor, MI, 1962), 1–3; Medoff, *Zionism and the Arabs*, 86.

6. Medoff, *Zionism and the Arabs*, 127–39.

7. For a brief biography, see "Eugene Kulischer," *Population Index* 22:2 (Apr. 1956): 100.

8. Kulischer, *Europe on the Move*, 25, 242–46, 324–25; Eugene M. Kulischer and A. J. Jaffe, "Notes on the Population Theory of Eugene M. Kulischer," *Milbank Memorial Fund Quarterly* 40:2 (Apr. 1962): 187–206; cf. Kulischer, *Jewish Migration—Past Experience and Postwar Prospects* (New York, 1943).

9. Schechtman's previous publications included works on Jewish autonomy, a history of anti-Jewish violence during the Russian civil

war, and a study of what he called the "Jewish irredenta" in the Middle East.

10. J. Schechtman, *European Population Transfers, 1939–1945* (New York, 1946), 451–52, 454; cf. the antitransfer arguments of the Princeton demographer Irene Taeuber, "Population Displacements in Europe," *Annals of the American Academy of Political and Social Science* 234 (July 1944): 1–12.

11. J. Schechtman and Y. Benari, *History of the Revisionist Movement*, vol. 1 (1925–30) (Tel Aviv, 1970).

12. L. Weinbaum, *A Marriage of Convenience: The New Zionist Organization and the Polish Government, 1936–1939* (Boulder, CO, 1993), chap. 8, 178.

13. H. Rosenblum, "Promoting an International Conference to Solve the Jewish Problem: The New Zionist Organization's Alliance with Poland, 1938–1939," *Slavonic and East European Review* 69:3 (July 1991): 478–501; J. Schechtman, *Fighter and Prophet: The Vladimir Jabotinsky Story*, vol. 2, *The Last Years* (New York, 1961), esp. 337.

14. V. Jabotinsky, *The Jewish War Front* (London, 1940), 28, 87, 187, 212.

15. Schechtman, *Fighter and Prophet*, 2:352–53.

16. D. Hacohen, "Ben Gurion and the Second World War: Plans for Mass Immigration to Palestine," *Studies in Contemporary Jewry* 7 (1991): 247–68; W. Roger Louis, *Imperialism at Bay: The United States and the Decolonization of the British Empire, 1941–45* (New York, 1978), 58–59.

17. R. Medoff, *Zionism and the Arabs*; on the broader transformation in Zionist thought, Y. Weitz, "Jewish Refugees and Zionist Policy during the Holocaust," *Middle Eastern Studies* 30:2 (Apr. 1994), 351–68.

18. H. Morgenthau, review of "Were the Minorities Treaties a Failure?" *Journal of Modern History* (1944): 236–37; on Morgenthau, see N. Guilhot, "The Realist Gambit: Postwar American Political Science and the Birth of IR Theory," *International Political Sociology* 2:4 (Dec. 2008): 281–304.

19. W. Friedmann, "The Disintegration of European Civilization and the Future of International Law," *Modern Law Review* (Dec. 1938): 194–214.

20. "International Law in Development: Discussion on the Redrafted Report of the Committee," *Transactions of the Grotius Society* 27 (Problems of Peace and War) (1941): 252–88.

21. Lemkin papers, unpublished memoir draft, New York Public Library.

22. A. Kochavi, *Prelude to Nuremberg: Allied War Crimes Policy and the Question of Punishment* (Chapel Hill, NC, 1998), 165–70, 222–30.

23. J. Cooper, *Raphael Lemkin and the Struggle for the Genocide Convention* (New York, 2008).

24. Ibid., 158–59.

25. H. Lauterpacht, *International Law and Human Rights* (New York, 1950), 35–36; M. Caloyanni, "Memorandum on International Criminal Legislation and Peace," *Revue Internationale de Droit Penal* 17 (1946): 305–32, and "Le proces de Nuremberg et l'avenir de la Justice penale international," *Revue de Droit International, de Sciences Diplomatiques et Politiques* 24 (Oct.–Dec. 1946): 174–82.

26. M. Siegelberg, "Contending with the Ghosts of the Past: Raphael Lemkin and the Origins of the Genocide Convention," *Columbia Undergraduate Journal of History* 1:1 (January 2006): 30–48.

27. N. Masalha, *The Expulsion of the Palestinians: The Concept of "Transfer" in Zionist Political Thought, 1882–1948* (Washington, DC, 1992); B. Morris, *The Birth of the Palestinian Refugee Problem Revisited* (Cambridge, 2004), 39–65.

28. R. Medoff, *Zionism and the Arabs*, 79–80; Morris, *Birth of the Palestinian Refugee Problem*, 43; R. Khalidi, *The Iron Cage: The Story of the Palestinian Struggle for Statehood* (Boston, 2006).

29. R. Medoff, *Zionism and the Arabs*, 104–5, 119–20; C. Weizmann, "Palestine's Role in the Solution of the Jewish Problem," *Foreign Affairs* 20:2 (1942): 324–38; Morris, *Birth of the Palestinian Refugee Problem*, 54–55.

30. R. Medoff, *Zionism and the Arabs*, 81–82, 115–17, 119–20.

31. Schechtman, *Fighter and Prophet*, 2:324–25; N. Masalha, *Expulsion of the Palestinian*, 29.

32. Medoff, *Zionism and the Arabs*, 125–26; Borgwardt, *A New Deal for the World*.

33. R. Medoff, *Militant Zionism in America: The Rise and Impact of the Jabotinsky Movement in the United States, 1926–1948* (Alabama, 2002), 214–15.

34. B. Morris, "Yosef Weitz and the Transfer Committee, 1948–49," *Middle East Studies* 22:4: 522–61, 530, 547; R. Medoff, *Zionism and the Arabs*, 149–51.

35. I. Claude, *National Minorities*, chap. 12.

36. J. Schechtman, *Population Transfers in Asia* (New York, 1949), 84–142, 84, 86, 131, 134; Schechtman, "Decline of the International Protection of Minority Rights," *Western Political Quarterly* 4:1 (March 1951): 1–11.

37. D. Armitage, *The Declaration of Independence: A Global History* (Cambridge, MA, 2007), 137. Despite arguments by scholars such as Hersch Lauterpacht that recognition was becoming a matter of collective decision under international law, in fact the League after 1919 had involved itself far more directly in the recognition of new states than the UN did. For the debate on this point in the late 1940s and the failure of Lauterpacht's neo-Grotian approach, see T. Grant, *The Recognition of States: Law and Practice in Debate and Evolution* (New York, 1999), 123–28.

38. The political weakness of pan-Africanism after independence is noted in D. E. Apter and J. S. Coleman, "Pan-Africanism or Nationalism in Africa," in *Pan-Africanism Reconsidered*, ed. S. Allen (Berkeley, 1962), 81–116; the transformation of the Middle East in B. Maddy-Weitzman, *The Crystallization of the Arab State System, 1945–1954* (Syracuse, 1993).

39. M. Dudziak, *Cold War, Civil Rights: Race and the Image of American Democracy* (Princeton, 2000), 44–45.

40. Hersch Lauterpacht, *International Law and Human Rights* (New York, 1950), 279.

CHAPTER 4
JAWAHARLAL NEHRU AND THE GLOBAL UNITED NATIONS

1. L. Goodrich, "From League of Nations to United Nations," *International Organization* 1:1 (Feb. 1947), 3–17; J. Kunz, "The Secretary-General on the Role of the United Nations," *American Journal of International Law* 52:2 (April 1958): 302.

2. E. Korovin, "The Second World War and International Law," *American Journal of International Law* 40:4 (Oct. 1946): 742–55.

3. R. H. Russell, *A History of the United Nations Charter: The Role of the United States, 1940–1945* (Washington, DC, 1958), 823–24; on the trusteeship system, L. Goodrich, E. Hambro, and A. P. Simons, *Charter of the United Nations: Commentary and Documents* (New York, 1969), chap. 12; populations in R. J. Kozicki, "The UN and Colonialism," in *The Idea of Colonialism*, ed. R. Strausz-Hope and Harry Hazard (New York, 1958), 383–430.

4. Katherine Courney cited in Birn, *League of Nations Union*, 223; Bidault in M. Dockrill, ed., *British Documents on Foreign Affairs* (hereafter *BDFA*), Part IV: series M [International Organisations, Commonwealth Affairs and General), vol. 1 (University Publications of America), 233. More broadly, E. J. Hughes, "Winston Churchill and the Formation of the United Nations Organization," *Journal of Contemporary History* 9:4 (Oct. 1974): 177–94, 188.

5. Welles, in N. Smith, *American Empire: Roosevelt's Geographer and the Prelude to Globalization* (California, 2004), 356.

6. P. Henshaw, "South African Territorial Expansion and the International Reaction to South African Racial Policies, 1939–1948," *South African Historical Journal* 50 (May 2004), 69–70; for African American reactions, cf. P. M. von Eschen, *Race against Empire: Black Americans and Anticolonialism, 1937–1957* (Ithaca, NY, 1997), 61.

7. Dockrill, ed. *BDFA*, IV, M v. 1, 247–49.

8. M. Crowder, "Tshekedi Khama, Smuts, and South-West Africa," *Journal of Modern African Studies* 25:1 (1987), 25–42, 42; P. Henshaw, "South African Territorial Expansion."

9. L. Lloyd, "'A Family Quarrel': The Development of the Dispute over Indians in South Africa," *Historical Journal* 34:3 (Sept. 1991): 703–25, 706; B. Pachai, *The International Aspects of the South African Indian Question, 1860–1971* (Cape Town, 1971), 26; Curtis in T. Gorman, "Lionel Curtis, Imperial Citizenship, and the Quest for Unity," *The Historian* 66 (2004): 83.

10. L. Lloyd, "'A Family Quarrel,'" 703–25.

11. Pachai, *International Aspects of the South African Indian Question*, 170–72.

12. *Collected Works of Mahatma Gandhi* (hereafter *CWMG*), 79: 16 July 1940–27 December 1940, 289.

13. *Harijan*, 13-10-1940, cited in *CWMG*, 79, 288–90.

14. *Bombay Chronicle* cited in C. Thorne, *The Issue of War: States, Societies, and the Far Eastern Conflict of 1941–1945* (London, 1985), 163. See too M. Lake and H. Reynolds, *Drawing the Global Colour Line: White Men's Countries and the International Challenge of Racial Equality* (Cambridge, 2008), chap.14.

15. E. Manela, *The Wilsonian Moment: Self-Determination and the International Origins of Anticolonial Nationalism* (Oxford, 2007); C. Aydin, *The Politics of Anti-Westernism in Asia: Visions of World Order in Pan-Islamic and Pan-Asian Thought* (New York, 2007); Thorne, *The Issue of War*, 178–79.

16. Documents in T. R. Sareen, ed., *Subhas Chandra Bose and Nazi Germany* (New Delhi, 1996), 311–17.

17. T. R. Sareen, "Subhas Chandra Bose, Japan, and British Imperialism," *European Journal of East Asian Studies* 3:1 (2004): 69–97.

18. "International Contacts," in *Essential Writings of J Nehru*, ed. S. Gopal and U. Iyengouri (Oxford, 2003), 200, and "India and the World" [1936], 206.

19. For a different interpretation of Nehru's international thought, see M. Bhagavan, "A New Hope: India, the United Nations, and the Making of the Universal Declaration of Human Rights," *Modern Asian Studies* (2008): 1–37; for an exploration of the domestic implication of Nehru's nationalism, see P. Chatterjee, "The Moment of Arrival: Nehru and the Passive Revolution," in his *Nationalist Thought and the Colonial World* (Minnesota, 1993), 131–67.

20. "A World Federation" [1939] *Essential Writings of J Nehru*, 216–17, and "A Real Commonwealth," ibid., 218–19; Gopal, ed., *Selected Works of J Nehru*, 1:443–44.

21. "Colonialism Must Go," in Gopal and Iyengouri, eds., *Essential Writings of J Nehru*, 222–25.

22. Gopal and Iyengouri, ed., *Selected Works of J Nehru*, 1:438–40. 450–51, 503.

23. Lloyd, "'A Family Quarrel,'" 718.

24. N. Mansergh, ed., *The Transfer of Power, 1942–47*, 12 vols. (London, 1970–1983), 8:21–22, 91, 139–41, 194.

25. John Darwin, "'A Third British Empire'? The Dominion Idea in Imperial Politics," *Oxford History of the British Empire* (Oxford, 1998), 66–86; see also L. Lloyd, "Britain and the Transformation from Empire to Commonwealth: The Significance of the Immediate

Postwar Years," *Round Table* 343 (July 1997): 333–60, and Lloyd with A. James, "The External Representation of the Dominions, 1919–1948: Its Role in the Unraveling of the British Empire," *British Year Book of International Law* (Oxford, 1997), 479–501.

26. Mansergh, ed., *Transfer of Power*, 8:400–401, 714–15, 849–52, 858–61.

27. Lloyd, "'A Family Quarrel,'" 719.

28. Ibid., 719–21.

29. Mansergh, ed., *Transfer of Power*, 7:771–772.

30. Pachai, *International Aspects of the South African Indian Question*, 191–92.

31. Russell, *History*, 908.

32. R. J. Moore, *Escape from Empire: The Attlee Government and the Indian Problem* (Oxford, 1983), 188–99. That the domestic jurisdiction clause was already clearly weaker than planned for the majority of General Assembly members could be seen in debate over whether to admit Franco's Spain. On whether the character of the regime precluded it being offered membership, see L. Goodrich, "The United Nations and Domestic Jurisdiction," *IO* 3:1 (Feb. 1949): 14–28; Pachai, *International Aspects of the South African Indian Question*, 192.

33. Gopal and Iyengouri, ed., *Selected Works of J Nehru*, 1:437.

34. Dockrill, *BDFA*, series IV, M, vol. 2 (2002): 281–87; Dockrill, *BDFA*, series IV, M, vol. 4 (2001): 115–17, 211; R. Wilson, "Some Question of Legal Relations between Commonwealth Members," *American Journal of International Law* 51:3 (July 1957): 611–17.

35. Lloyd, "'A Family Quarrel,'" 724; Lloyd, "'A Most Auspicious Beginning": The 1946 United Nations General Assembly and the Question of the Treatment of Indians in South Africa," *Review of International Studies* 16:2 (April 1990): 153.

36. Gopal and Iyengouri, ed., *Selected Works of J Nehru*, 1:468.

37. W. K. Hancock and J. van der Poel, eds., *Selections from the Smuts Papers* (Cambridge, 1973), 6:16, 20, 33.

38. Ibid., 46–47 [3/46], 80.

39. Ibid., 101, 111–13 [27/10.46] 12/46, 120–30.

40. Government of India, Ministry of External Affairs, *Question of the Treatment of Indians of South Africa before the United Nations: Verbatim Record of 106th to 112th Meetings of the First Committee held in November 1947* (New Delhi, 1948), 25–28, 45–47, 75–76.

41. Ibid., 13–19, 120–21.

42. Dockrill, ed., *BDFA*, series M, vol. 5 (2002), 237.

43. T. Hovet, *Africa in the United Nations* (Evanston, IL, 1963), 8.

44. Pachai, *International Aspects of the South African Indian Question*, 259.

45. Deshingkar, "Construction of Asia in India," 176–78; G. Krishna, "India and the International Order: Retreat from Idealism," in *The Expansion of International Society*, ed. H. Bull and A. Watson (Oxford, 1984), 269–89.

46. For an illuminating case study of the transformed role of international anticolonialism, see M. Connelly, *A Diplomatic Revolution: Algeria's Fight for Independence and the Origins of the Post–Cold War Era* (Oxford, 2002).

Afterword

1. S. Tetsua, "The Political Discourse of International Order in Modern Japan, 1868–1945," *Japanese Journal of Political Science* 9:2 (2009), 233–49, 239.

2. W. Roger Louis, *Imperialism at Bay* (Oxford, 1978), 247.

3. Bevin in M. Dockrill, ed., *BDFA*, series IV: M, 2, 214–15, 237–42.

4. G. Kennan, *Memoirs (1925–1950)* (New York, 1969), 229–32; for a critique of the American attempt to use the UN, see H. Morgenthau, "The New United Nations and the Revision of the Charter," *Review of Politics* 16:1 (Jan. 1954): 3–21.

5. Cited in Thomas Knock, *To End All Wars: Woodrow Wilson and the Quest for a New World Order* (Princeton, 1992), 272–74; on Rusk, D. Rusk, *As I Saw It* (New York, 1990).

6. An early study is L. Sohn, "Expulsion or Forced Withdrawal from an International Organization," *Harvard Law Review* 77:8 (Jun. 1964): 1381–1425.

7. A. J. Hotz, "The United Nations since 1945: An Appraisal," *Annals of the American Academy of Political and Social Science* 336 (July 1961): 134.

8. H. Bull, "What Is the Commonwealth?" *World Politics*: 577–87, 579.

Index §

Bentham, Jeremy, 67
Bernadotte, Folke, 138
Bevin, Ernest, 99, 177, 185, 196
Biafra, 146
Bidault, Georges, 151
Big Four, 168
Big Three, 16, 28, 63–65, 133, 164, 194, 196, 202. *See also* great powers
Bill of Rights, international. *See* International Bill of Human Rights
Biltmore conference (1942), 136
biological weapons, 3
Boer War, 17, 18, 30, 31, 33, 34, 35, 47, 69, 74
Bombay Chronicle (newspaper), 163–64
Bondelzwaarts massacre, 51
Borgwardt, Elizabeth, 138
Bose, Subhas Chandra, 165–67, 169
Bosnia, 148
Boutros-Ghali, Boutros, 1, 4
Bowman, Isaiah, 15, 111–12, 115, 119
Bretton Woods system, 10
British Empire/Britain: ancient Greece as model for, 69–71, 75–78, 85–86; and domestic jurisdiction, 176; and founding of UN, 13–15, 17–18; and imperialism, 52–53, 151, 172; India and, 78, 89, 91, 160–67, 171–78; and internationalism, 32–33, 36–41, 66–67, 191–92; and Jewish resettlement, 106, 118, 121; leadership role of, 21, 37, 70, 85–86, 92; and League of Nations, 13–15, 21, 79, 84–86, 90–91, 192; as model for world community, 85, 90–92, 192; and Palestine, 106, 118, 134, 144, 152; and population transfer, 134; and race, 91,

159–60, 172, 192–93; and South Africa, 30, 35, 52–53, 153–56, 186; and UN, 30–31, 155–57; U.S. relations with, 20–21, 36, 38, 45, 59, 84–86, 172; Zimmern and, 89–92, 95. *See also* commonwealth
British Royal Air Force, 30
Bureau of Economic Warfare, 125
Burma, 180
Bush, George H. W., 5
Bush (George W.) administration, 2–6, 10, 12, 102

Cambodia, 148
Canada, 35, 76, 77, 172, 178
Carnegie Endowment, 125
Carr, E. H., *Twenty Years' Crisis*, 94
Cassin, Rene, 6
Cecil, Robert, 41, 42, 44
Central Europe, 104–5
Chamberlain, Houston, 47
Charter of the United Nations: contradictory elements in, 202; domestic jurisdiction reservation in, 176; drafting of, 15, 28, 61–62; interpretations of, 8; and national sovereignty, 25; and use of force, 198. *See also* preamble to UN Charter
China, 3, 100, 152, 180, 187, 188
Christianity, 22, 58, 72, 93
Churchill, Winston, 10, 16, 41, 55, 58–60, 151, 166
citizenship, world, 80
civilizing mission, 20–21, 33, 35, 48–49, 52–53, 65, 74, 78, 82, 85–88. *See also* European civilization; Western civilization
Claude, Inis, 207n11
Clinton administration, 2

flexibililty of, 191, 194; founding of, 1, 6–10, 14–17, 28, 58–65, 190–91; as global forum, 153, 188–89; historiography of, 5–9; ideals of, 188–90, 198; League of Nations and, 14–16, 59–60, 65, 142–43, 149–51; membership of, 145, 198–99; missions of, 1–2, 191; models proposed for, 15; perspectives on founding of, 6–10, 190–91; post-imperial, 195–203; purpose of, 27, 104, 189; recognition of new states by, 145, 220n37; reform proposals for, 3, 202–3; survival of, 202; technical agencies of, 202; unifying character of, 199–200; War Crimes Commission, 127. *See also* Charter of the United Nations; General Assembly; preamble to UN Charter; Security Council

United States: ancient Greece as model for, 96, 98; anticolonialism of, 152, 195; British Empire's relations with, 20–21, 36, 38, 45, 59, 84–86, 172; and domestic jurisdiction, 176; exceptionalism in, 99; and founding of UN, 14–17; and Genocide Convention, 132; and human rights, 131; and imperialism, 44, 99, 103, 150, 152, 157, 198; and India, 166, 178, 184; and internationalism, 31, 83; and Israel, 198; leadership role of, 23, 92, 95, 99–103, 110, 166; and League of Nations, 86; and minority rights, 147; and Palestine, 144; and refugee crisis, 24, 106, 110; and South Africa, 186; and UN, 2–4, 12–13, 22, 61–62, 99–101, 197–98; USSR and, 189; Zimmern and, 95–97, 99–102

Uniting for Peace, 197
Universal Declaration of Human Rights, 8, 129–33, 142
Universal Postal Union, 80
U.S. Department of War, 127
U.S. State Department, 14, 58, 99
USSR. *See* Union of Soviet Socialist Republics
utopianism, 6

Vandenburg, Arthur, 16
Victorian mentality, 21, 23, 55, 69, 70, 98, 101, 123
Vietnam, 187

Wallace, Henry, 125, 137–38
war crimes, 127
Warburg, Felix, 135–36
Wavell, Percival, Lord, 161, 171, 172, 175, 180
Webster, Charles, 7, 15, 63–64
Weitz, Yosef, 139
Weizmann, Chaim, 134, 135, 137
Welles, Sumner, 152
Wells, H. G., 52, 84
Were the Minority Treaties a Failure?, 122
Western civilization, 99. *See also* civilizing mission; European civilization
Whitman, Walt, 64
Williams, John Fischer, 98
Wilson, Woodrow: and ethical governance, 74, 79; Fourteen Points, 43, 55; and internationalism, 12–13, 42–46, 98, 188; and League of Nations, 42–46, 84; and national self-determination, 43, 81; Smuts and, 20, 38, 42, 44–45
Wise, Stephen, 134, 135
Woodward, Edward, 99